Building Land and Estates

To our daughters
Deborah, Sara and Georgina

Building Land and Estates

their acquisition and
development

Second edition

Ian G C Stratton LL B
Solicitor

Oyez Longman

© Oyez Longman Publishing Limited 1983
21/27 Lamb's Conduit Street
London WC1N 3NJ

ISBN 0 85120 696 4

First published 1979
Second edition 1983

Set in Baskerville
and printed in Great Britain by
Butler & Tanner Ltd, Frome and London

Contents

Preface

The subject of private residential housing and the attendant social and economic problems are never far from the headlines. In the past few years the fortunes of the building industry have been cyclical: first came a boom with builders paying inflationary prices for land, speculators making vast profits, and purchasers queueing to buy houses; then the slump and the consequential liquidation or bankruptcy of developers, with banks and mortgagees rushing to enforce their securities and houses standing built but unsold. Recently there has been a substantial increase in housing 'starts', but there are now warning signs there may be a levelling off in activity. To counteract these extreme fluctuations political and fiscal solutions have been attempted which have further complicated an already complex situation. Moreover, since building land is a shrinking national asset it is unlikely that such difficulties will be eased in the future.

Given this turbulent background, it is essential for the harassed practitioner to keep a cool and analytical mind when consulted by his client, whether a builder or a purchaser of a new dwellinghouse. The aim of this book, therefore, is threefold: first, to identify the problems and pitfalls arising on the acquistion of land for residential building, and to suggest solutions to such problems (Chapters 1–3); secondly, to deal with the various methods of disposal of individual new properties on a basis which is fair to both builder and purchaser (Chaper 4); and thirdly to consider other related topics involving building land (Chapters 5–10).

Since the last edition, apart from a considerable number of important cases, the Community Land Act 1975 has been repealed and the Highways Act 1980 and the Local Government Planning and Land Act 1980 have become law. As a result fairly extensive alterations to the text have been necessary and in addition a new chapter entitled 'Building Regulations' has been included. It has, however, only been possible to make very brief reference to taxation matters and the reader is referred to the standard works on this topic for more detailed information.

An attempt has been made to present the law as it stood on 31 August 1983 according to sources available at the time. However, no statement in this book is to be construed as a recommendation or advice to be acted upon.

Harrogate
31 August 1983   I G C Stratton

Table of Cases

Table of Statutes

xvi

Table of Statutory Instruments

Chapter 1

Modes of Acquisition of Building Land

1 General

As a result of complex planning, fiscal, and other considerations it may not always be possible to employ the usual straightforward conveyancing formalities when purchasing an undeveloped parcel of building land. For example, the land may have planning potential but no existing consent, and the builder may wish to acquire the land subject to planning consent being obtained. He will, therefore, seek advice on the type of contract which will provide the best method of dealing with the problem. The difficulties which may need to be resolved before a purchaser commits himself to outright acquisition of building land are innumerable as will be seen from later chapters: acquisition of easements for services; removal of restrictive covenants; closure of roads; problems with footpaths; acquisition of other land for assembly of the site, are but a few of the contingencies which can arise. This chapter, therefore, considers the various methods of acquiring building land so as to deal with such difficulties.

2 Option

An option to purchase land is granted where there is an offer to sell by the grantor which such grantor cannot contractually withdraw during the prescribed period for which the offer remains open to be accepted by the grantee. For a more extensive definition see *Griffith* v *Pelton* [1958] Ch 205 at p 225. The arrangement falls within s 40 of the Law of Property Act 1925, and must, therefore, be evidenced in writing.

From the grantee's, or prospective purchaser's, point of view an option is the most satisfactory method of tying up land for a specified period without committing himself to purchase, as it allows flexibility. Conditional contracts, which are discussed generally at head 4 below, differ from options in this respect since once the condition upon which the contract is based has been fulfilled the purchaser will almost certainly be obliged to complete the purchase, even if circumstances may meanwhile have changed, thus possibly rendering the deal less attractive than originally envisaged.

It is usual for an option fee to be payable and this is a matter of commercial negotiation between the parties. A nominal consideration will be sufficient as in *Mountford* v *Scott* [1975] Ch 258 where an option was granted for a pound. Where no consideration is given the agreement must be under seal. As to capital gains tax payable on an option fee, see *Randall* v *Plumb* [1975] 1 All ER 734 and *Strange* v *Openshaw* (*Inspector of Taxes*) [1983] STC 416.

It is obviously generally in the grantor's interest to restrict the period of the option to as short a time as possible, but if a long term option is granted regard should be had to s 9(2) of the Perpetuities and Accumulations Act 1964 which provides that options to purchase land for valuable consideration (other than options to purchase reversions on leases: s 9(1)) should be limited to a period of twenty-one years. However, under the 'wait and see' rule contained in s 3(3) an option which prima facie offends s 9(2) will be saved if it is exercised within the twenty-one year perpetuity period: failure to exercise within that period renders the option void thereafter. As to where third parties intervene, and the rule against perpetuities is infringed, see s 10 of the 1964 Act.

Since the grantee can assign the benefit of the option by express assignment, or implication, and the assignee can enforce the option against the original grantor, the owner of the land may find himself dealing with a different purchaser if the option is exercised. His solicitor should therefore consider inserting a provision against assignment when drafting the option. An option may not be assignable if it is personal to the grantee (*Griffith* v *Pelton* [1958] Ch 205).

Unless provision is made to the contrary, an option, when exercised, creates an open contract (*Re Crosby's Contract* [1949] 1 All ER 830). It is, therefore, prudent to incorporate the National, the Law Society's or other standard conditions of sale in the option agreement. Furthermore, a clause should be included that the grantor will deduce a good and marketable title of at least fifteen years. If possible it is wise to investigate the grantor's title prior to entering into the agreement. In the event of the option being exercised the purchase price of the land should be specifically defined or an effective mechanism for ascertaining such price incorporated in the option agreement even though the court can substitute its own mechanics for fixing the price if the obstruction of one party prevents the intended system from operating (*Sudbrook Trading Estate Ltd* v *Eggleton* [1982] 3 WLR 315, HL).

Special considerations apply when an option is granted by a trustee or a tenant for life. By s 51(1)(2) and (3) of the Settled Land Act 1925 a tenant for life may at any time either with or without consideration, grant by writing an option of settled land at a price fixed at the time of the granting of the option provided that such option is exercisable within ten years, and the price, having regard to all the circumstances, is the best that can reasonably be obtained. The consideration for the grant of an option is capital money (s 51(5)). Section 28(1) of the Law of Property Act 1925 as amended gives to trustees all the powers of a tenant for life. Similarly, by s 39 of the Administration of Estates Act 1925 personal representatives have the powers of a tenant for life and trustees for sale and can therefore grant an option. The personal representatives of the deceased grantor will be bound by the terms of the option unless it provides to the contrary, or the option is merely a personal covenant of the grantor (*Kennewell* v *Dye* [1949] Ch 517).

Extreme care should be taken when exercising an option to purchase since the terms for exercising the option must be strictly complied with. For example, it must be exercised within the period of the option (*Riddell* v *Durnford* [1893] WN 30). An option can be extended but such extension must be evidenced in writing and all other relevant formalities complied with. Failure by a solicitor to comply with the relevant formalities in serving a notice exercising an option to purchase can constitute negligence (*Roberts* v *J W Ward & Son* (1982) 126 SJ 120, CA). The practitioner should therefore look ahead and carefully consider the procedure for exercising the option when drafting the agreement. Where no method of exercise was laid down it was held in *New Hart Builders Ltd* v *Brindley* [1975] Ch 342 that s 196 of the Law of Property Act 1925 was applicable and the notice must be in writing; oral exercise was insufficient unless accepted by the grantor. Compare *Yates Building Co Ltd* v *R J Pulleyn & Sons (York) Ltd* (1975) 119 SJ 370.

For a precedent of an option to purchase freehold land see the Appendix.

3 Pre-emption

An option must be distinguished from 'a right of pre-emption' whereby a prospective purchaser will have the first opportunity to buy certain land *in the event* of the owner deciding to sell. For an example of where an option was distinguished from a right of pre-emption see *Du Sautoy* v *Symes* [1967] Ch 1146. A right of pre-emption (unlike an option) does not create an interest in land, but merely a contractual right (*Pritchard* v *Briggs and Others* [1980]

Ch 338). Again a time limit on the exercise of the right should be imposed, and on the expiration of such period the purchaser's rights will be extinguished, and the owner will be able to dispose of the land as he thinks fit. Such an uncertain arrangement is usually not satisfactory for a builder.

4 Conditional contract

It is usually easy to distinguish a conditional contract from an option, but in cases of doubt the Court will look at the substance of the document not the form: see *Re Longlands Farm, Long Common, Botley Hants, Alford* v *Superior Developments Ltd* [1968] 3 All ER 552. A conditional contract offers a builder client little flexibility since once the condition has been fulfilled he will almost certainly be obliged to complete the transaction. Consideration should be given to whether the condition in such a contract should take the form of a condition precedent or a condition subsequent. In the former case the parties may only become liable if the condition is fulfilled, while in the latter case the contract is immediately binding and in the event of the condition not being fulfilled the contract may cease to have effect, or a party may have the right to rescind. Such factors can be of importance in ascertaining whether there has been a disposal of the land for tax purposes, and when such disposal became effective.

When drafting the condition particular care must be taken to define what precisely is intended by the parties and to foresee, as far as possible, what events will occur and to provide for such events. For example, an agreement should not state simply that it is conditional upon planning permission being obtained. Specific reference should be made to either outline or detailed planning permission: see *Hargreaves Transport Ltd* v *Lynch* [1969] 1 All ER 455. Furthermore, planning permission may be granted *but* subject to conditions which involve the purchaser in additional expense and accordingly, are unsatisfactory (see *Richard West & Partners (Inverness) Ltd* v *Dick* [1969] 2 Ch 424). Therefore, the contract should set out the rights of the parties in the event of such contingency arising. Other drafting points for consideration where the agreement is to be conditional on the granting of planning permission are, for example: who makes the application for planning permission; whether an appeal is to be undertaken; if so what type of appeal; who is to conduct and meet the expense of such appeal. Each case will depend on its facts and it is impossible to anticipate all eventualities. Nevertheless it must be emphasized that the practitioner should give careful consideration to all the factors involved to define as specifically as possible the rights and duties of the parties. Additional care at this stage may avoid litigation.

A condition may remain unsatisfied for a long time during which circumstances change. For example, a builder client may not be prepared to wait any longer for a condition about planning permission to be fulfilled and may require to purchase land on a speculative basis. The question then arises as to whether he can do so and waive the condition. In *Heron Garage Properties Ltd* v *Moss* [1974] 1 WLR 148 the contract was conditional upon planning permission being obtained within a specified time. Such permission was not obtained and the purchaser endeavoured to waive the condition. It was held that no unilateral waiver was possible in the circumstances. On the facts of the case the condition was not exclusively for the benefit of the purchaser since the vendor owned adjoining land which was benefited by the condition. To avoid the consequences of this decision a specific clause can be inserted in the agreement reserving to the purchaser the right to waive the condition.

For precedents of clauses of conditions precedent and subsequent on outline planning consent being obtained see the Appendix.

5 Tender

Where building land is offered for sale by tender it is the tender itself which constitutes the offer, not the invitation to tender, and there is no binding contract until the tenderee has communicated his acceptance to the tenderor (*Spencer* v *Harding* (1870) LR 5 CP 561). The tenderee is not obliged to accept the highest tender, and normally the invitation to tender will contain a provision to that effect. When acting for the builder client, it must be remembered that if an unqualified tender is submitted and accepted there will usually be an immediate binding contract. The invitation itself, however, may indicate that no legally binding agreement is envisaged.

Therefore, the invitation to tender and the development brief must be perused and discussed with the client's other technical advisers to ensure that there is nothing prejudicial affecting the land and that the technicalities of the arrangement are understood. If the tenderee's solicitors agree, it is advisable to raise enquiries before contract in the usual manner. It may also be possible to ascertain the type of offer the tenderee has in mind, as, for example, in the case of a lease, whether he requires a ground rent or a premium. If the builder client is not satisfied, it may be advisable to qualify the tender in regard to some aspect, or alternatively, to submit the whole tender 'subject to contract', thus leaving the matter open as a basis for future negotiation. However if all the terms of the tender are defined in the tender document it is too late for the tenderee to incorporate the words 'subject to contract' in his acceptance as there is no scope for any further formal contract (*Michael Richards Properties Ltd* v *Corporation of Wardens of St Saviour's Parish, Southwark* [1975] 3 All ER 416). Nevertheless, it would seem that the circumstances where the words 'subject to contract' are meaningless will have to be exceptional (*Duttons Brewery Ltd* v *Leeds City Council* (1982) 261 EG 885, CA). Furthermore in the case of continuing negotiations the words 'subject to contract' can only be removed if both parties agree that they should be expunged or if such agreement must necessarily be implied (*Cohen* v *Nessdale Ltd* [1982] 2 All ER 97, CA). The decision as to whether to submit a qualified tender is a commercial one, but the client should be advised of the alternatives available.

6 Auction

The vendor's solicitors will prepare the sale particulars and conditions. Any advertisement of the auction usually contains a provision that such conditions and particulars can be inspected at the offices of the vendor's solicitors or agents. The prospective purchaser's solicitor should take this opportunity to confirm that there is nothing prejudicial affecting the land. Subject to the co-operation of the vendor's solicitors enquiries before contract can be raised in the usual manner.

When preparing or approving the auction particulars the Sale of Land by Auction Act 1867 should be borne in mind. Section 5 provides that the particulars or conditions of sale by auction of any land shall state whether it will be sold without reserve, or subject to a reserved price, or whether a right to bid is reserved; if it is stated that the land will be sold without reserve, or to that effect, then it shall not be lawful for the seller to employ any person to bid at the sale, or for the auctioneer knowingly to take any bidding from any such person. Further, by s 6 of the Act where any sale of land by auction is declared, either in the particulars, or conditions of sale, to be subject to a right for the seller to bid, it is lawful for the seller or any one person on his behalf to bid.

Accordingly, the rights to reserve a price and to bid must be incorporated in the auction particulars, and will often be included by reference to the standard conditions of sale, as, for example, Condition 1(2) of the National Conditions of Sale 20th Ed. Also Condition 25(2), (3) of the Law Society's Conditions of Sale (1980 Ed).

At the auction the auctioneer may seek to alter or vary the particulars and conditions orally. If such alterations are clear and distinct the purchaser will be bound by them even if he did not hear them (*Re Hare and O'More's Contract* [1901] 1 Ch 93). However, to avoid uncertainty it is advisable to incorporate any such alterations or corrections into the written agreement prior to signature.

The bid constitutes the offer and there is no binding contract until the auctioneer accepts the final bid by banging the hammer (*McManus* v *Fortescue* [1907] 2 KB 1). A written contract will then be entered into by the parties to satisfy the requirements of s 40 of the Law of Property Act 1925. The auctioneer can sign the contract as agent for both the vendor and the purchaser (*Cohen* v *Roche* [1927] 1 KB 169). Such signature on behalf of the purchaser must, however, be immediate, or as soon after the fall of the hammer as possible, to form part of the transaction (*Chaney* v *Macklow* [1929] 1 Ch 461). Each case will, however, depend on its facts. For example, compare *Matthews* v *Baxter* (1873) 28 LT 669 with *Bell* v *Balls* [1897] 1 Ch 663.

7 Registration of the agreement

In the case of an option, conditional contract, or right of pre-emption the grantee or purchaser must effect registration at the appropriate registry. For a recent example of the registration of an option taking priority over the prior registration of a right of pre-emption, see *Pritchard* v *Briggs and Others* [1980] Ch 338, CA. As to registration pursuant to a priority notice see Chapter 3, head 2.

If the agreement relates to unregistered land it should be registered as an estate contract, C(iv), at the Land Charges Registry. Failure to register will result in the agreement being void against a purchaser of the legal estate for money or money's worth: see Land Charges Act 1972, s 2(4)(iv) and s 4(6). 'Money or money's worth' can mean even a purchase at an undervalue (*Midland Bank Trust Co Ltd* v *Green* [1981] AC 513). If the grantor has sold the land to a third party and the contract is unregistered the grantee will have a right of action for damages for breach of contract against the grantor (*Wright* v *Dean* [1948] Ch 686). Such damages may extend to the loss of profit on a proposed development if the grantor was aware of the circumstances at the time the option was granted (*Cottrill* v *Steyning & Littlehampton Building Society* [1966] 1 WLR 753). This remedy and the resultant litigation may not, however, impress the client if the land is required to build up his land bank, or if the grantor has no money and is unable to pay the damages.

Similarly, in the case of registered land the agreement should be registered. Registration is by way of notice or caution or restriction at the Land Registry: see ss 49(1)(*c*), 59(2), 54 and 58(1) of the Land Registration Act 1925. See also *Registered Land Practice Notes*, 1982/83, L1: Options and other estate contracts.

For the solicitor's duty as to registration in both contract and tort, see *Midland Bank Trust Co Ltd and Another* v *Hett, Stubbs and Kemp* [1979] Ch 384.

8 Stamp duty

If no consideration is payable for the grant of an option the agreement will be under seal and attract the fixed duty of fifty pence (Stamp Act 1891, Sched 1). However, in *George Wimpey & Co* v *IRC* [1975] 2 All ER 45 a written agreement, whereunder, in consideration of the payment of the sum of £15,000, an option to purchase land was granted, was held to be a conveyance on sale and attracted ad valorem stamp duty under s 54 of the Stamp Act 1891. A certificate for value should therefore be included in an option agreement, when appropriate. No duty will be payable on a conditional agreement under hand.

Chapter 2

Enquiries Before Contract

1 Services

(a) General

It is essential when a building estate is proposed to ensure that adequate services are available. It is therefore prudent to locate the public services, and inform the client. He will then be able to judge, with the assistance of his technical advisers, the suitability of such services, and perhaps more important, the cost involved to make the services available for the proposed new dwellings. Furthermore, consideration should be given to any easements, whether existing or to be acquired, passing through the land of a third party which are necessary to connect the development to the public services.

(b) Foul and surface water

Section 37(1) of the Public Health Act 1936 relates to new buildings and provides that where plans of a building are, in accordance with building regulations, deposited with a local authority (the district council) the authority shall reject the plans unless: (*a*) the plans show that satisfactory provision will be made for the drainage of the building; or (*b*) the authority are satisfied that in the case of the particular building they may properly dispense with any provision for drainage. 'Drainage' includes the conveyance, by means of a sink and any other necessary appliance, of refuse water and the conveyance of rain water from roofs. By s 37(2) there is a right to apply to a court of summary jurisdiction for determination of a dispute arising under the section.

Section 37(3) provides that a proposed drain will not be satisfactory unless it is proposed to be made, either to connect with a sewer, or to discharge into a cesspool or into some other place. This is subject to the proviso that the drain shall not be required to be made to connect with a sewer unless: (*a*) that sewer is within one hundred feet of the site of the building, and is at a level which makes it reasonably practicable to construct a drain to communicate with it, and, if not a public sewer, is a sewer which the person constructing the drain is entitled to use; and (*b*) the intervening land is land through which that person is entitled to construct a drain. By s 37(4) the local authority may require a drain to be made to connect with a sewer more than one hundred feet away but which is otherwise such a sewer as is mentioned in subs (3) provided that the authority undertake to bear so much of the expenses reasonably incurred in constructing, and maintaining and repairing, the drain as may be attributable to the fact that the distance to the sewer exceeds one hundred feet. Again if there is a dispute as to the amount of any payment to be made an application can be made to the court of summary jurisdiction for arbitration.

Under s 16(1)(*b*) and (3) of the Water Act 1973 the water authority must provide a public sewer for domestic purposes if the owners of premises who propose to erect new buildings on the premises require for their drainage a sewer communicating (how and where the authority consider appropriate) with a private sewer provided by the owners, and the owners undertake to meet any relevant deficit. The duty to provide a sewer pursuant to s 16 does not arise until planning consent for development has been granted (*George Wimpey & Co v Secretary of State for the Environment and Maidstone District Council* [1979] 2 CLJ 231). However, the statutory duty placed upon the water authority can extend to the provision of a pump and rising main so as to enable the private sewer to communicate with the public sewer (*William Leech (Midlands) Ltd v Severn-Trent Water Authority* (1981) 260 EG 1123, CA).

Section 34 of the Public Health Act 1936 gives owners and occupiers rights to drain into public sewers within their district. The section provides that the owner or occupier of any premises, or the owner of any private sewer, within the district (now the area covered by the water authority: s 14(2)(*a*) of the Water Act 1973) shall be entitled to have his drains or sewer made to communicate with the public sewers provided that the sewage system generally would not be prejudiced. However, where separate public sewers are provided for foul water and for surface water there is no right to discharge (*a*) foul water into a sewer provided for surface water, or (*b*) (except with the approval of the authority) surface water into a sewer provided for foul water. Nor is there a right to communicate with a storm water overflow sewer. For the formalities in regard to the exercise of the right to drain into the public sewers, see s 34(3). As to the right of the water authority itself to make the connection with the public sewers and to require a contribution towards the costs thereof, see s 36(1), (2) and (3) of the 1936 Act.

Clearly as much information as possible about the drainage of both foul and surface water from a proposed building estate should be obtained and given to the client. Useful preliminary information as to the availability of a public sewer and any potential liability for maintenance under s 24 of the Public Health Act 1936 can be gained from enquiry 5 of the standard form of local search (Oyez form Con 29, 1982 Edition). Particular attention should be paid to the reply to enquiry 5 of the form as to whether there is any liability under ss 12 and 13 of the Public Health Act 1961 which relate to the recovery of the construction cost of sewers. It should, however, be noted that as the sewerage function has now passed from the local authority to the regional water authority the former may not have up-to-date information. Further enquiries may therefore be required of the appropriate water authority. Furthermore, by s 32 of the Public Health Act 1936 the water authority is under a duty to keep at their offices for inspection (by any person, at all reasonable hours, free of charge) a map showing and distinguishing all public sewers and drains within their district. Where some of the sewers are for foul or surface water exclusively the map will show this (s 32(2)). See also circular 94/69: Surface water run off from development. By s 35 of the Agriculture (Miscellaneous Provisions) Act 1968 the water authority is required to have for public inspection a register containing details of the drainage hereditaments in their area and also a map.

The drainage rights specifically revealed by the draft contract should be scrutinized, and the question of maintenance and the size of pipe are particularly relevant. Surface water leaves a completed development much faster than a green field site. Therefore, bigger drains may be needed, and a new easement may have to be negotiated. In addition to specifically negotiated easements, easements may be acquired (inter alia) by prescription under the doctrine of *Wheeldon* v *Burrows* (1879) 12 ChD 31, or by s 62(1) of the Law of Property Act 1925 which provides that a conveyance of land shall be deemed to include and shall convey (inter alia) all ditches, ways, waters, watercourses, liberties, privileges, easements, rights and advantages whatsoever appertaining or reputed to appertain to the land at the time of the conveyance. The section is subject to any contrary intention shown in the conveyance (s 62(4)). The position may also be affected by the special conditions of sale, eg condition 5(3) of the Law Society's General Conditions of Sale (1980 Ed).

(c) Adoption of sewers

Both the builder and the purchaser of a newly constructed dwelling will require the estate sewers to be adopted and maintained at the public expense. By s 18(1) of the Public Health Act 1936 a developer may enter into an agreement with the appropriate water authority to construct a sewer or sewage disposal works, which, if completed in accordance with the terms of the agreement, will be adopted by the water authority. Alternatively after the construction of the sewers the owner can make an application to the water authority pursuant to s 17(2) of the Public Health Act 1936 for a declaration that the sewers have been vested in the water authority. Section 17(4) provides that a water authority in deciding whether to accept such adoption shall have regard to all the circumstances of the case, and in particular whether the sewers are adapted to or required for the general sewerage system; whether the sewer is constructed under a highway; the number of buildings served or to be served; and the method of construction and state of repair of the sewers. An owner aggrieved by the refusal of the water authority to make a declaration has a right of appeal to the minister, see s 17(3).

(d) Water supply

Section 137(1) of the Public Health Act 1936 (as amended by s 29 of the Water Act 1945 and Sched 8 para 41 of the Water Act 1973) deals with the supply of water to new houses. It provides that where plans of a house are deposited with a local authority, the authority shall reject the plans unless there is a satisfactory proposal for the provision of a wholesome domestic water supply, either (a) by connecting the house to a supply in pipes provided by the statutory water undertakers, or (b) where this is not reasonably possible, by otherwise taking water into the house through a pipe, or (c) if, in all the circumstances, neither of the preceding alternatives can reasonably be required, by providing a supply of water within a reasonable distance of the house. The authority must be satisfied that the proposals can and will be carried into effect. In cases of dispute there is a right of application to a court of summary jurisdiction.

By s 137(2), if after any such plans have been passed, it appears to the local authority that the proposal has not been carried out, or has not resulted in a satisfactory water supply being provided, the authority shall give notice to the owner of the house prohibiting him from occupying it, or permitting it to be occupied, until the authority are satisfied that a satisfactory supply has been made available. Again in the case of a dispute, there is a right of application to a court of summary jurisdiction.

Section 37(1) of the Water Act 1945, as amended by the Housing Act 1949, s 46, deals with the duty of the water authorities to provide a domestic water supply for new buildings. It provides that where it is proposed to erect new buildings on land for which a domestic water supply is needed the owner (as defined by s 59(1)) may require the authority to construct any necessary service reservoirs, to lay the mains so that the buildings can be connected at a reasonable cost, and to supply water to those mains. Under the proviso to s 37(1) the authority may impose on the owner certain conditions, namely: (*a*) it may require him to undertake to pay, in respect of each year, a sum amounting to one eighth of the expense of providing and constructing the necessary service reservoirs, and providing and laying the necessary mains (less amounts received by the authority in respect of water supplied, whether for domestic purposes or non-domestic purposes, in that year from those mains) until the aggregate amount of water rates payable annually in respect of the buildings, when erected, and in respect of any other premises connected with the mains equals or exceeds such sum, or until the expiration of twelve years, whichever first occurs; and (*b*) (except in the case of a local or public authority) it may require the owner to deposit with the water authority as security for payment of the annual sums, such sum, not exceeding the total expense of constructing the service reservoirs and providing and laying the mains, as the authority may require. Interest is payable on the deposit, and the sum so deposited may be used to pay any capital payment due (s 37(2)). The section does not define the expression 'service reservoir and mains'. For the meaning of 'necessary drains' see *Cherwell District Council* v *Thames Water Board* [1975] 1 All ER 763 and *Royco Homes Ltd* v *Southern Water Authority* [1979] 3 All ER 803, HL.

Section 37(4) of the 1945 Act provides that if the water authorities do not fulfil their obligations under the section they will be guilty of an offence. However, the water authorities have a defence if they are prevented from fulfilling their obligations by unavoidable accident or other unavoidable cause.

For a precedent of a requisition to supply water under s 37 and an agreement made pursuant to this section, see *The Encyclopaedia of Forms and Precedents*, 4th Ed, vol 23, pp 103 and 104.

(e) Gas and electricity

By the Gas Act 1972, Sched 4, para 2(1), if premises are within twenty-five yards of a gas main an owner can require a supply from the British Gas Corporation. Under Sched 4, para 2(2) the person requiring the supply will have to meet the cost of providing and laying the pipe to the extent that though it may not run over his land it extends thirty feet from the main. Reasonable notice must be given and a person may be required to give an undertaking to pay the appropriate charges and to give security (Sched 4, para 2(5)). Furthermore, by s 1 of the Gas Act 1980 the supply of gas to any premises in excess of 25,000 therms a year is to be subject to the special agreement of the Corporation or liable to special rates of charge.

By para 27(1) of the Schedule to the Electric Lighting (Clauses) Act 1899 the owner or occupier of any premises within fifty yards of any distributing main can demand a supply from the appropriate area board. The board may, however, require the owner to pay the cost of so much of the electric line as may be laid on his property, and also of so much of the line laid more than sixty feet from any distributing main although not on his property.

(f) Access

It is crucial to the development of a building estate that there is adequate road access to the nearest public highway. For an example of the difficulties arising where no right of access existed, see *Perry v Stanborough (Developments) Ltd and Wimborne District Council and Dorset County Council* (1977) 244 EG 551: a strip of land intervened between the development and the public highway, and the court held that there was no duty upon the planning authority or the highway authority to acquire the strip compulsorily, and the matter was one for private negotiation between the adjoining owners. As to the circumstances under which an easement of necessity will arise, see *Nickerson* v *Barraclough* [1981] 2 WLR 773, CA. The reply to enquiry 1 of the standard form of local search will reveal whether the roadways abutting on to the premises are maintainable at the public expense, and provide additional detailed information. If, however, there is some doubt as to where the nearest public highway is, enquiries can be made of the appropriate highway authority; by s 36(6) of the Highways Act 1980 there is a duty on the authority to keep a list available for inspection of the streets maintainable at public expense.

If access to a public highway is given by a specific right of way over land in the ownership of a third party, the precise terms of the right, as revealed by the draft contract, should be examined to ensure that there is a valid and subsisting easement. The terms must be such as to allow the purchaser and his successors in title to use the right to give access to a residential estate. In particular, it must not be limited to a specific class of person or type of vehicle. A grant of a right of way for carriages will allow it to be used for motor cars (*White* v *Grand Hotel Eastbourne Ltd* [1913] 1 Ch 113). Each case will depend on its own circumstances but relevant considerations are the use of the land which the right serves, and the surrounding land and buildings. It is, therefore, desirable that the grant be couched in the widest possible terms: see *Robinson* v *Bailey* [1948] 2 All ER 791. However, even a right in wide terms does not authorise an excessive user: see *Jelbert* v *Davis* [1968] 1 WLR 589. If there is a possibility that the proposed user may be excessive it may be necessary to renegotiate the terms of the grant. For a precedent of a right of way over a private road see *The Encyclopaedia of Forms and Precedents*, 4th Ed, vol 7, p 670.

The question of liability to maintain the right of way or private road is also relevant. Difficulties can arise as a result of damage caused by construction traffic pending completion of the development. In the absence of specific provision, there is no implied obligation on either party to maintain the right of way: *Duncan* v *Louch* (1845) 6 QB 904. As regards damage to the surface of a road caused by excessive user see *Weston* v *Lawrence Weaver Ltd* [1961] 1 QB 402.

However, problems in connection with rights over access roads should now be considered in the light of the case of *Bracewell* v *Appleby* [1975] Ch 408. An estate comprised six houses served by a private access road over which the six householders each had a right of way. The defendant purchased one of the houses with the benefit of a right of way over the access road. He then purchased a second plot without rights over the access road and commenced to build a house. The plaintiffs sued for damages and an injunction. As the plaintiffs had delayed enforcing their rights until the building was almost complete damages in lieu of an injunction were granted. Such damages were assessed on the basis the plaintiffs would have been willing to accept a fair sum for loss of amenity and increased use of the private road but a sum that would not have been so great that the defendant would have been deterred from building the house. Compare *Wrotham Park Estate Co Ltd* v *Parkside Homes Ltd* [1974] 1 WLR 798 and *Wakeham* v *Wood* (1982) 43 P & CR 40, CA (see head 3(*a*) below) in regard to restrictive covenants.

2 Parcels and plan

The purchase price of building land is often calculated by multiplying the number of acres to be purchased by a specific cash sum per acre. It is therefore necessary to have carefully drafted parcels in the contract which enable the acreage to be accurately ascertained. The written description of the property contained in the parcels should be such as to allow the purchaser clearly to identify the property. The parcels may have become obsolete over the years and if so should be updated. The phrase 'for building purposes' should not be used to describe the land when no valid planning consent is in existence since it may give rise to the implication that such consent exists. For information as to the description of parcels in the case of registered land see s 76 of the Land Registration Act 1925.

It is advisable, if not essential, to have a detailed description of the land by reference to a plan. Indeed a purchaser can insist on a plan unless the description of the property in the contract is sufficient (*Re Sansom and Narbeth's Contract* [1910] 1 Ch 741 at p 749). The plan should be attached to the document and signed by the parties. Where the written description of the property is uncertain and there is an unambiguous plan the latter will prevail (*Wallington* v *Townsend* [1939] Ch 588). Reference to a plan 'for the purposes of identification only' should be avoided unless the parcels are absolutely accurate (see *Neilson* v *Poole* (1969) 210 EG 113). See also *Moreton C Cullimore (Gravels)* v *Routledge* (1977) 121 SJ 202 where it was held that a plan 'for the purposes of identification only' did not control the parcels in the body of the conveyance, but was to be used to see where the land was situate and not to define its measurements. Plans marked 'for the purpose of identification only' are also unacceptable to the Land Registry. (See further *Registered Land Practice Notes*, 1982/83, C 1: Requirements for plans in dispositions of registered land). The effect of stating that the plan is 'for the purpose of delineation only' is to indicate that it is not true to scale (*Re Freeman and Taylor's Contract* (1907) 97 LT 39). It was held in *Whitehouse* v *Hugh* [1906] 2 Ch 283 that although the land was sold for building purposes, and by reference to a plan which showed proposed roads on adjacent land, there was no liability on the vendor to make up such roads.

With registered land difficulties will not arise when there is a purchase of the whole of the land comprised in the title and there is a filed plan. However, in many cases there will be a sale of part of the land comprised in a registered title, and then an accurate description and plan will be required as in the case of non-registered conveyancing.

In conclusion, therefore, the parcels clause should be clear and comprehensive, and from the purchaser's point of view make reference to a plan for the purpose of admeasurement. Such a reference may not, however, be acceptable to a cautious vendor. Measurements should be shown on the plan or included by reference to a scale. The compass points should be marked. The site should also be inspected to confirm that the boundaries coincide with the parcels and plan, and if necessary surveyed. Inspection may also reveal other rights and matters which may not be immediately apparent from the terms of the draft contract and plan. See also Chapter 4, head 2, 'The estate plan'.

3 Restrictive covenants

(a) General

A covenant which prohibits building or otherwise restricts the user of land can obviously sterilize the land for building purposes. Restrictive covenants are strictly construed; hence a covenant 'not to erect an unseemly building' was held to be too vague and was unenforceable (*Murray* v *Dunn* [1907] AC 283). However, a covenant for the benefit of both the vendor and the purchaser that a piece of land should not be built on is enforceable (*McLean* v *McKay* (1873) LR 5 PC 327). Furthermore, a covenant restricting the use of land to one house was held enforceable when a breach of such covenant would have resulted in an increase in the use of the roadway serving the land (*Re Gadd's Land Transfer* [1966] Ch 56). In the case of a covenant to submit plans, failure to submit such plans will probably result only in an award for nominal damages although if such plans would not have been approved then an injunction may result (*Goolden* v *Anstee* (1868) 18 LT 898). If building work has not commenced the covenantee's remedy will be an injunction, although damage must be proved.

However, the position in relation to covenants against building has been affected by the case of *Wrotham Park Estate Co Ltd* v *Parkside Homes Ltd* [1974] 1 WLR 798. Land was subject to a covenant not to be developed except in strict accordance with a layout plan to be submitted and approved. The land was sold at auction to the defendants, and reference was specifically made in a special condition to the covenant which was registered as a land charge, class D(ii). The defendants in deliberate breach of the covenant built fourteen houses, but took the precaution of taking out an insurance indemnity policy insuring each property for £20,000. The court held the defendants were bound by the covenant but refused to grant a mandatory injunction. Instead, damages were awarded on the basis of 5 per cent of the defendants' profits as a quid pro quo for relaxing the covenant. The decision, however, does not help a builder who has just commenced construction in breach of covenant and is served with an injunction. Nor does it assist a less audacious client who may not be able to risk the trouble and expense of litigation. It is significant in the *Wrotham Park* case that the builders took out an insurance indemnity policy. (See also *Shaw* v *Applegate* [1977] 1 WLR 970 where damages were awarded rather than an injunction.)

If, however, there is a flagrant breach of a restrictive covenant by a builder the court may, rather than award damages, grant a mandatory injunction requiring the demolition of the offending building (*Wakeham* v *Wood* (1982) 43 P & CR 40, CA). Very careful consideration should therefore be given to all relevant circumstances before commencement of building on land subject to covenants which restrict, prohibit or inhibit residential development. Prudence may dictate an application be made to the Lands Tribunal for the discharge or modification of the covenants pursuant to s 84 of the Law of Property Act 1925 (see (*g*) below).

(b) Insurance indemnity policies

Where difficulties arise in connection with restrictive covenants, as, for example, where it is not possible to ascertain the persons presently entitled to the benefit of such covenants, or there is uncertainty as to whether the covenants have been released under the doctrine of waiver, or otherwise, the quickest solution is usually to arrange an insurance indemnity policy against any loss arising from the enforcement of the covenants. A policy will avoid the trouble and expense of an application to the Lands Tribunal or the courts (see (*g*) below). Advice as to the availability and premiums payable for such a policy should be obtained from an insurance broker as there are few companies willing to undertake business of this kind. Each case will depend on its own circumstances and the amount of money at risk. With a large building estate the capital involved, and loss of profit on the development if prevented, could be substantial. Usually the more modern a covenant is, the more difficult it will be to arrange cover. The insurance company will often make extensive enquiries through solicitors and surveyors in the locality as to the history of the covenant and the land on which it is imposed before deciding whether to underwrite the risk. Moreover the problems of obtaining an insurance policy have been further aggravated by *Federated Homes Ltd* v *Mill Lodge Properties Ltd* [1980] 1 All ER 371, CA, where it was held in the case of a post-1926 restrictive covenant which relates to or touches and concerns the covenantee's land, that the effect of s 78(1) of the Law of Property Act 1925 is to annex the covenant to the covenantee's land (whether or not the covenant contains words of annexation) the benefit of which covenant will run with the land and be available to the covenantee's successors in title. When approving the terms of the draft insurance indemnity policy, care should be taken to ensure that it enures for the benefit not only of the successors in title of the insured, but also mortgagees. For a precedent of a proposal form for such a policy and the policy itself see *The Encyclopaedia of Forms and Precedents*, 4th Ed, vol 13, pp 392 and 394.

(c) Specific release

When the parties entitled to the benefit and subject to the burden of a restrictive covenant are clearly identifiable, and both wish to lift the covenant, the simplest method of proceeding is by a specific deed of release. For a precedent of such release see *The Encyclopaedia of Forms and Precedents*, 4th Ed, vol 17, p 583.

In the case of registered land, it will be necessary to lodge at the Land Registry the deed of release together with a certified copy, the land certificate of the land burdened, and the appropriate fee. Before the entry of the restrictive covenants on the register can be cancelled it will be necessary for the applicant to prove that the deed of release is fully effective. As has been seen, in practice, this can be extremely difficult, and is sometimes impossible, to establish. In such circumstances, the Chief Registrar will enter a notice of the deed on the register: such notice does not, however, operate as a cancellation of the entries. Similar considerations will apply with non-registered land.

If there is any doubt as to whether a deed of release effectively releases or modifies a restrictive covenant additional protection may be obtained by means of an insurance indemnity policy (if available) or an application to the Lands Tribunal to discharge the covenant (see (*g*) below).

(d) Waiver and acquiescence

A person entitled to the benefit of a restrictive covenant may lose his right to enforcement if there has been a continuing breach of a substantial nature (*Osborne* v *Bradley* [1903] 2 Ch 446). For the doctrine of waiver and acquiescence to be effective the person entitled to the benefit of the covenant must have knowledge of the breach (*Knight* v *Simmonds* [1896] 2 Ch 294; and see *Shaw* v *Applegate* [1977] 1 WLR 970). There is a useful presumption in the case of a continued and open breach of more than twenty years where a waiver or release will be presumed (*Hepworth* v *Pickles* [1900] 1 Ch 108). In practice, the doctrine may give rise to evidential uncertainty and it may be advisable to obtain an insurance indemnity policy, or make an application to the Lands Tribunal for discharge (see (*g*) below).

(e) Change in the character of the area

The position is succinctly summarised in a passage from the judgment of Farwell J in *Chatsworth Estates Co* v *Fewell* [1931] 1 Ch 224 at pp 229 and 230:

> The defendant's first ground of defence is that there has been such a complete change in the character of the neighbourhood, apart from the plaintiff's acts and omissions, that the covenants are now unenforceable. But to succeed on that ground the defendant must show that there has been so complete a change in the character of the neighbourhood that there is no longer any value left in the covenants at all ... so that an action to enforce them would be unmeritorious, not bonafide at all, and merely brought for some ulterior purposes.

Again evidential uncertainty can arise in practice and it may be advisable to take out an insurance indemnity policy or make an application to the Lands Tribunal for discharge (see *(g)* below).

(f) Unity of seisin

Where the land burdened and the land benefited by the restrictive covenant become vested in the same person, the covenant will be extinguished and will not automatically revive on subsequent severance unless the common owner then re-creates them (*Re Tiltwood, Sussex; Barrett* v *Bond and Others* [1978] Ch 269).

(g) Section 84 of the Law of Property Act 1925 (as amended)

There is a statutory power to vary or discharge restrictive covenants by way of an application to the court or the Lands Tribunal. This is contained in s 84 of the Law of Property Act 1925, as amended by s 28 of the Law of Property Act 1969. The procedure involved can be lengthy, expensive and fraught with the usual hazards of litigation; it will not, therefore, recommend itself to an anxious client who requires a quick and inexpensive solution to the problem of a restrictive covenant. Such a course will usually only be adopted when it is not possible to remove a covenant in any other way or obtain an appropriate insurance indemnity policy.

Section 84, as amended, is set out in the Third Schedule to the Law of Property Act 1969 and the reader is referred to the Schedule for details of the powers of the Lands Tribunal to order wholly or partially the discharge or modification of a restrictive covenant pursuant to s 84(1). Further, subss (1A),(1B) and (1C) were added as a result of s 28(2) of the Law of Property Act 1969 and widen the effect of the original s 84(1). For the further powers of the court to decide whether land is affected by a restrictive covenant and as to the construction of an instrument imposing such a covenant see s 84(2). Section 84 applies whether or not the document imposing the restriction is produced to the court or the Lands Tribunal (s 84(6)). Section 84(12) deals with leaseholds (except mining leases) and provides that where a term of more than forty years is created (whether before or after commencement of the Act) the section shall, after the expiration of twenty-five years of the term, apply to restrictions affecting the land in the same way as if the land had been freehold.

(h) Other statutory powers

When land is acquired from a local authority there is a useful, but often overlooked, power to override any restrictive covenants which may affect the land. The power is given by s 127(1) of the Town and Country Planning Act 1971 which protects the local authority and anyone who derives title from the authority provided that the land has been acquired or appropriated for planning purposes by the local authority and there is no breach of planning permission. Compensation may be payable (see subs (3)) by the local authority who, in turn, may call for an indemnity (see subs (4)). For the general effect of the section see *Dowty Boulton Paul* v *Wolverhampton Corporation (No 2)* [1976] Ch 13.

With regard to flats s 165 of the Housing Act 1957 allows the county court on the application of a local authority, or a person interested in a house, to vary a restriction that a house shall be used as a single private dwellinghouse by permitting it to be converted into flats. The section will apply where because of changes in the character of the neighbourhood it would be possible to let the premises as flats but not as a single dwellinghouse, or where planning permission has been granted for the conversion into two or more dwellings.

4 Planning permission

(a) General

A solicitor is under a duty not only to investigate the legal title to land, but also to ascertain what planning provisions and restrictions affect the land, and to advise his client accordingly (*Lake* v *Bushby and Another* [1949] 2 All ER 964). If there is no valid planning consent in existence for residential development, useful information can be gleaned from the replies to local searches and any other additional enquiries made of the local planning authority. The result of such enquiries may be of assistance to a builder client when assessing his chances of obtaining planning permission in respect of land being acquired speculatively. For example, the replies will reveal existing consents or whether the property is situate in the green belt. When there is a written planning permission for residential development the document must be perused and a copy sent to the client and his architect. In particular the planning consent must not have expired and be free from any unduly onerous conditions whether imposed by statute or otherwise. These matters are discussed in the next three sections.

(b) Duration of planning permissions

Section 41(1) of the Town and Country Planning Act 1971 provides that planning permissions, whether actual or deemed shall be granted subject to the condition that development must be begun not later than the expiration of – (a) five years, beginning with the date on which permission is granted or deemed to be granted; or (b) such other period which the planning authority considers appropriate. A condition that the development must be begun not later than five years from the date of the grant is deemed to be included in a planning permission even if no express provision is made to that effect (s 41(2)). Section 41(3) contains certain exceptions and, in particular, the provisions relating to outline permission.

Section 42(1) provides that 'outline planning permission' means planning permission granted, in accordance with the provisions of a development order, with the reservation for subsequent approval by the local planning authority, or the Secretary of State, of 'reserved matters' not particularised in the application. Section 42(2) goes on to provide that where outline planning permission is granted for development the following conditions shall apply:

(a) . . . in the case of any reserved matter, application for approval must be made not later than the expiration of three years beginning with the date of the grant of outline planning permission; and

(b) . . . the development to which the permission relates must be begun not later than whichever is the later of the following dates—
(i) the expiration of five years from the date of the grant of outline planning permission; or
(ii) the expiration of two years from the final approval of the reserved matters, or, in the case of approval on different dates, the final approval of the last such matter to be approved.

Such conditions are deemed to be included in the planning permission even if there is no express provision to that effect (s 42(3)). Furthermore, by s 42(4) the authority concerned may substitute, or direct that there be substituted, for the periods of three years, five years or two years, referred to in subs (2), such other periods respectively (whether longer or shorter) as they consider appropriate. By s 42(5) different periods may be allocated to different parts of a development. Section 43(1) provides that for the purposes of ss 41 and 42 development shall be taken to be begun on the earliest date on which any specified operation comprised in the development begins to be carried out. Specified operation is defined by s 43(2) as meaning any of the following: (*a*) any work of construction in the course of the erection of a building; (*b*) the digging of a trench which is to contain the foundations, or part of the foundations, of a building; (*c*) the laying of any underground main or pipe to the foundations of a building or to any such trench as is mentioned in (*b*) above; (*d*) any operation in the course of laying out or constructing a road or part of a road; (*e*) any change in the use of any land, where that change constitutes material development (as defined by s 43(3)). The 'pegging out' of lines for part of a new estate road is a specified operation so as to constitute development within s 43(2) (*d*) (*Malvern Hills District Council* v *Secretary of State for the Environment and Another* (1982) 262 EG 1190, CA). For other provisions as to the duration of planning permissions granted prior to 1 April 1969 see the Town and Country Planning Act 1971 Sched 24 paras 18 to 22.

Development carried out in contravention of the statutory conditions imposed by ss 41 and 42 is treated as not authorised by the planning permission (whether outline or other) and an application for approval of a reserved matter as not made in accordance with the condition (s 43(7)). Where by virtue of ss 41 and 42 a development is subject to a condition that the development to which the permission relates must be begun before the expiration of a particular period and that development has been begun within that period but the period has elapsed without the development having been completed, see s 44 which gives the local planning authority powers to terminate a planning permission by reference to a time limit. In particular, s 44(2) provides that if the local planning authority are of the opinion that the development will not be completed within a reasonable period, they may serve a 'completion notice' stating that the planning permission will cease to have effect at the expiration of a further period specified in the notice, being a period of not less than twelve months after the notice takes effect. A completion notice will be revealed by the replies to the local search (see Oyez form Con 29, 1982 Ed, Pt II, enquiry VI).

(c) *Conditions*

By s 29(1) of the Town and Country Planning Act 1971 the local planning authority may impose such conditions on a planning permission as they think fit. (See also circular 5/68, 'The use of conditions in planning permissions'.) By s 30(1) of the 1971 Act specific conditions may be imposed on the granting of a planning permission: (*a*) for regulating the development or use of any land under the control of the applicant (whether or not it is land in respect of which the application was made) or requiring the carrying out of works on any such land, so far as appears to the local planning authority to be expedient for the purposes of or in connection with the development authorised by the permission; (*b*) for requiring the removal of any buildings or works authorised by the permission, or the discontinuance of any use of land so authorised, at the end of a specified period, and the carrying out of any works required for the reinstatement of land at the end of that period. Where a planning permission is granted subject to a condition mentioned in s 30(1)(*b*) a planning permission is 'planning permission granted for a limited period' (s 30(2)). By s 30(3) where (*a*) planning permission is granted for development consisting of or including the carrying out of building or other operations subject to a condition that the operation shall be commenced not later than a time specified in the condition (not being a condition attached to the planning permission by or under ss 41 or 42 of the Act); and (*b*) any building or other operations are commenced after the time so specified, the commencement and carrying out of those operations do not constitute development for which that permission was granted. Such a condition is particularly important for builders. A condition may be ultra vires or void for uncertainty. As to the rules governing whether a condition is ultra vires, see *Fawcett Properties Ltd* v *Buckingham County Council* [1961] AC 636. An example of such a condition is seen in *R* v *Hillingdon London Borough Council, ex parte Royco Homes Ltd* [1974] QB 720 where a local planning authority was held to exceed its powers in imposing a condition that the development of houses should be occupied by persons on the council house waiting list, and requiring security of tenure for the occupants of such houses for a period of twelve years. It should be noted that if there is a fundamental condition which is ultra vires it will almost certainly render the planning consent as a whole void (see the *Hillingdon London Borough Council* case above).

(d) Section 52 agreements

In addition to conditions being imposed by statute, or specifically by a local planning authority, such an authority may require even stricter control over a development by means of a 'section 52 agreement'. Section 52(1) of the Town and Country Planning Act 1971 provides that a local planning authority may enter into an agreement with any person interested in land in their area for the purpose of restricting or regulating the development or use of the land, either permanently or during such period as may be prescribed by the agreement; and any such agreement may contain such incidental and consequential provisions (*including provisions of a financial character*) as appear to the local authority to be necessary or expedient for the purposes of the agreement. Such an agreement is enforceable by the local authority against the successors in title of the interested persons (s 52(2)). The circumstances in which a local planning authority will require a s 52 agreement are varied, for example the phasing of a development, the construction of access or infrastructure works, and the acquisition by the local authority of a planning gain. A s 52 agreement cannot, however, impose a fetter on the subsequent exercise of other statutory powers (*Windsor and Maidenhead Royal Borough Council* v *Brandrose Investments Ltd* [1983] 1 All ER 818,CA). See also s 52 (3).

A s 52 agreement should be registered at the local land charges registry or as a D(ii) land charge and will be revealed by the appropriate searches. A copy of such agreement should be obtained from the vendor's solicitors and carefully considered as it may (inter alia) contain onerous liabilities of a *financial* character which could affect the viability of a building development. For a precedent of a s 52 agreement see *The Encyclopaedia of Forms and Precedents*, 4th Ed, vol 22, p 1102. As to the incorporation of positive covenants in such agreements, see s 33 of the Local Government (Miscellaneous Provisions) Act 1982.

If a prospective developer finds the provisions of an existing s 52 agreement obsolete or unacceptable, the Lands Tribunal have jurisdiction to hear an application for discharge or modification of the offending agreement pursuant to s 84 of the Law of Property Act 1925 (*Beecham Group Ltd's Application* (1980) 256 EG 829).

(e) Determination whether planning permission required

As will be seen from the above, the rules relating to planning permissions are complex and may well give rise to cases of doubt and uncertainty. In such circumstances the 1971 Act lays down a procedure for determining whether planning permission is required. Section 53(1) enacts that if any person who proposes to carry out any operations on land, or to make any change in the use of land, wishes to have it determined whether the carrying out of those operations, or the making of that change, would constitute or involve the development of the land, and if so, whether an application for planning permission is required, he may, either as part of an application for planning permission, or without any such application, apply to the local planning authority to determine that question. For application procedure, see the Town and Country Planning General Development Order 1977 (SI 1977 No 289), art 6(2).

5 Vacant possession and tenancies

(a) General

It is obviously preferable to purchase building land with vacant possession. If a contract makes no reference to tenancies and none are revealed on inspection, vacant possession will be implied (*Cook v Taylor* [1942] Ch 349); but to avoid doubt, a specific provision should be written in the agreement. The position may be covered by standard conditions of sale, as for example special condition F of the Law Society's Contract of Sale (1980 Ed) and special condition C of the National Conditions of Sale (20th Ed).

If the draft contract reveals tenancies full details should be obtained to ascertain firstly how and to what extent the land is affected, and secondly whether it is possible to obtain vacant possession, and if so, when. A sitting tenant of even part of building land can sterilize a proposed development, eg if site access is blocked. If the lease is long term and there is a lengthy residue unexpired a formal surrender will have to be negotiated. Of course, even though the lease has expired a tenant may have statutory security of tenure and certain grounds for possession may have to be established. A brief resumé of the types of protected tenancy most likely to affect land being purchased for building development follows.

(b) Business tenancies

The grounds on which a landlord may oppose an application by a tenant to renew a tenancy under the Landlord and Tenant Act 1954, Pt II, are set out in s 30. Assuming the tenant is not in breach of the terms of the lease there are two likely grounds on which the landlord may oppose an application for a new tenancy and obtain vacant possession.

First, that the landlord has offered, and is willing to provide, or secure, the provision of alternative accommodation for the tenant. The terms on which the alternative accommodation is available must be reasonable having regard to the terms of the current tenancy and to all other relevant circumstances, and the accommodation and the time at which it will be available must be suitable for the tenant's requirements (including the requirement to preserve goodwill) having regard to the nature and class of his business and to the situation and extent of, and facilities afforded by, the holding (s 30(1)(d)).

Secondly, that on the termination of the current tenancy the landlord intends to demolish or reconstruct the premises comprised in the holding, or a substantial part of those premises, or to carry out substantial work of construction on the holding or a part of it and that he could not reasonably do so without obtaining possession (s 30(1)(*f*)). The landlord must show a genuine intention to demolish and reconstruct at the time of the hearing (*Betty's Cafés Ltd v Phillips Furnishing Stores Ltd* [1959] AC 20). Entry into a building lease whereby the lessees undertake to carry out the work is sufficient intention (*Gilmour Caterers Ltd v Governors of St Bartholomew's Hospital* [1956] 1 QB 387). The landlord will have to show his ability to carry out the work by, for example, obtaining planning permission or establishing his financial competence. For an example of the latter see *Re St Martin's Theatre, Bright Enterprises Ltd v Willoughby de Broke* [1959] 3 All ER 298. For possession of part of the holding or provisions as to access or facilities for the landlord to carry out the works see s 31A, as added by s 7 of the Law of Property Act 1969.

No reference has been made to the complex procedural provisions affecting this topic as laid down by the Landlord and Tenant Act 1954, Pt II, and the reader is referred to the appropriate standard works. For compensation payable see s 37 of the Act.

(c) The Rent Act 1977

Assuming the tenant has observed the terms of the tenancy the most likely ground for obtaining possession of a dwellinghouse which is protected by the Rent Act 1977, and forms part of a building site, is to satisfy the court that suitable alternative accommodation is available for the tenant or will be available for him when the order for possession takes effect (Rent Act 1977 s 98 (1)(*a*)).

A certificate of the housing authority for the district in which the dwellinghouse is situated certifying that the authority will provide suitable alternative accommodation for the tenant by a date specified in the certificate is conclusive evidence of alternative accommodation (Rent Act 1977, Sched 15, Pt IV, para 3). Otherwise it is necessary to satisfy the conditions laid down by the Rent Act 1977, Sched 15, paras 4–6.

(d) Agricultural holdings

By s 1(1) of the Agricultural Holdings (Notices to Quit) Act 1977 a notice to quit an agricultural holding or part of an agricultural holding shall (notwithstanding any provision to the contrary in the contract of tenancy of the holding) be invalid if it purports to terminate the tenancy before the expiration of twelve months from the end of the current year of the tenancy. Certain exceptions to the general rule are set out in s 1(2). In particular s 1(1) does not apply to a notice given in pursuance of a provision in the tenancy agreement authorising the resumption of possession of the holding or part of it for some specified purpose other than agriculture (s 1 (2) (*b*)).

Furthermore, restrictions are imposed on the operation of notices to quit which give an agricultural tenant considerable security of tenure. Section 2(1) of the 1977 Act states that where a notice to quit an agricultural holding or part of an agricultural holding is given to the tenant and not later than one month from the giving of the notice the tenant serves on the landlord a counter notice in writing requiring that the subsection shall apply to the notice to quit, then the notice to quit shall not have effect unless the Agricultural Lands Tribunal consent.

Section 2(2) and (3) sets out certain circumstances when s 2(1) will not apply. The exception most likely to arise in the case of agricultural land required for building purposes is contained in s 2(3) Case B where the notice to quit is given and is stated to be given on the ground that the land is required for a use, other than for agriculture for which planning permission has been granted or for which permission is not required. As to the tenant's right to contest the reason stated under a notice served pursuant to Case B and to have the matter referred to arbitration, see the Agricultural (Arbitration on Notices) Order 1978 (SI 1978 No 257), Pt III. For the right to and measure of compensation for disturbance see s 34 of the Agricultural Holdings Act 1948 and ss 9 and 10 of the Agriculture (Miscellaneous Provisions) Act 1968 as amended by the Agricultural Holdings (Notices to Quit) Act 1977, Sched 1.

When acquiring agricultural land an enquiry should be made as to whether there is an existing notice to quit. Such notice may be rendered of no effect by the sale of the landlord's interest, or part of his interest, unless the tenant's consent is obtained: see further s 7 of the Agricultural Holdings (Notices to Quit) Act 1977.

The granting of a *licence* to occupy land (whether or not the agreement expressly so provides) in contemplation of the use of the land only for grazing or mowing during some specified period of a year is outside the provisions of the Agricultural Holdings Act 1948 (proviso to s 2(1)). For an example see *Reid* v *Dawson* [1955] 1 QB 214 where the period was for three hundred and sixty-four days.

(e) Licences

If the draft contract reveals that land is subject to a licence the terms of the document purporting to grant such licence must be considered with extreme care since a lease may have been created. The distinction between a lease and licence has always been a fruitful source of litigation and only a brief guide can be given here. McNair J laid down useful guidelines in relation to such distinction in *Finbow* v *Air Ministry* [1963] 1 WLR 697 at p 706 as follows:

(i) that the agreement must be construed as a whole, and that the relationship is determined by law and not by the label which the parties put on it, though the label is a factor to be taken into account in determining the true relationship;

(ii) that the grant of exclusive possession, if not conclusive against the view that there is a mere licence as distinct from a tenancy, is at any rate a consideration of the first importance;

(iii) that in all cases where the occupier has been held to be a licensee there has been something in the circumstances, such as a family arrangement, an act of friendship or generosity, or such like, to negative any intention to create a tenancy. In such circumstances it would be obviously unjust to saddle the owner with a tenancy. See further Denning LJ in *Facchini* v *Bryson* [1952] 1 TLR 1386 at p 1389.

If, therefore, the document purporting to be a licence contains words or clauses usually associated with a lease very careful consideration should be given to confirm that a lease has not been granted. See, for example, *Addiscombe Garden Estates Ltd* v *Crabbe* [1958] 1 QB 513.

(f) Allotment gardens

Section 22(1) of the Allotments Act 1922 defines 'allotment garden' as an allotment, not exceeding forty poles in extent, which is wholly or mainly cultivated by the occupier for the production of vegetable or fruit crops for consumption by himself or his family. As no trade or business is carried on on an allotment garden it will not constitute an agricultural holding, and will not be subject to the Acts regulating such tenancies. With reference to the grounds for possession of an allotment garden s 1(1) of the 1922 Act, as amended by s 1(1) of the Allotments Act 1950, provides that where land is let for use as an allotment garden, or is let to a local authority or association for the purpose of being sublet for such use, the tenancy of the land, or any part, shall not be terminable by the landlord by notice to quit or re-entry, notwithstanding any agreement to the contrary, except (inter alia) by:

(a) a twelve months or longer notice to quit expiring on or before 6 April or on or after 29 September in any year; or

(b) re-entry, after three months' previous notice in writing to the tenant, under a power of re-entry contained in or affecting the contract of tenancy on account of the land being required for *building*, mining or any other industrial purpose, or for roads or sewers necessary in connection with any of those purposes.

The above grounds for possession are not comprehensive but are those most likely to be applicable in the case of land required for building purposes.

The statutory grounds of possession supersede all terms of the tenancy agreement as, for example, in *Wombwell UDC* v *Burke* [1966] 2 QB 149, where it was held that a twelve month period of notice of termination applied rather than a six month termination provided by the tenancy agreement.

For the right to challenge a notice in certain circumstances see s 11 of the Allotments Act 1922, as amended by s 9 of the Allotments Act 1925. Compensation on quitting an allotment garden may be payable pursuant to s 2 of the 1922 Act, as amended by s 2 of the 1950 Act. For assessment and recovery of compensation see s 6 of the 1922 Act. Section 3 of the 1950 Act deals with compensation for disturbance.

6 Drainage easements

Section 25(1) of the Public Health Act 1936 enacts that where plans of a building or an extension to a building are, in accordance with building regulations, deposited with a local authority, and it is proposed to erect the building or extension over any sewer drain which is shown on the map of public sewers, the authority shall reject the plans, unless they are satisfied that in the circumstances of the particular case they may properly consent to the erection of the proposed building or extension, either unconditionally or subject to compliance with any requirements specified in their consent. In the case of dispute there is a right to apply to a court of summary jurisdiction for determination (s 25(2)). Thus it may be necessary to have such sewers or drains diverted or re-routed where they cross a building site.

Where, therefore, the draft contract reveals private drainage easements these may be required to be diverted or extinguished, eg by a deed of release (see s 52(1) of the Law of Property Act 1925), unity of seisin or implication. The grantee's title to the easement should be investigated to confirm the release is effective. In cases of doubt an insurance indemnity policy should be considered. Mere non-user is not conclusive evidence that the right of drainage has been extinguished (*Ward* v *Ward* (1852) 7 Exch 838). Where land is acquired from a local authority assistance may be obtained from statute as, for example, ss 118 and 127 of the Town and Country Planning Act 1971.

7 Private rights of way

If a right of way is revealed it may be necessary to have it diverted or extinguished by deed of release under seal (s 52(1) of the Law of Property Act 1925), unity of seisin or implication. The grantee's title to the right should be investigated to confirm the release is effective. Alternatively, the right may be extinguished by implication. A factor in deciding whether a right of way has been so extinguished is non-user, although this of itself may not be sufficient (*James* v *Stevenson* [1893] AC 162). In cases of doubt an indemnity insurance policy should be considered. Where land is acquired from a local authority assistance may be obtained from statute as, for example, ss 118 and 127 of the Town and Country Planning Act 1971. Section 214 of the 1971 Act makes provision for the extinguishment of *public* rights of way over land held by a local authority for planning purposes.

8 Road closure and diversion orders

(a) General

Recently there has been an increasing emphasis on urban renewal, as opposed to the development of green field sites for residential building. Such a trend will give rise to increasing problems where land required for building purposes is crossed by a public highway. A closure or diversion order can be made under the Town and Country Planning Act 1971 by an application to the Secretary of State, or, by an application to the magistrates' court under the Highways Act 1980. Which method is adopted will depend on the circumstances, but the planning procedure does envisage development taking place as a result of a planning permission, whereas the grounds under the Highways Act make no specific reference to those circumstances. The closure of a public highway or right of way does not operate to extinguish any private rights which cross the land: see *Wells* v *London Tilbury and Southend Railway Co* (1877) 5 Ch 126. Such private rights will have to be dealt with separately.

(b) The Highways Act 1980

By s 116(1) of the Highways Act 1980 if it appears to a magistrates' court, that a highway (not being a trunk road or a special road) is unnecessary, or can be diverted so as to make it nearer or more commodious to the public, the court may by order authorise it to be stopped up or diverted. Section 116(8)(*a*) provides that an order will not be made unless the written consent of the local planning authority (if not the applicants) and of every person having a legal interest in the land over which the highway is to be diverted is produced to and deposited with the court. Section 116(8)(*b*) goes on to provide that the order shall not authorise the stopping up of any part of the highway until the new part to be substituted for the part to be stopped up has been completed to the satisfaction of the court.

Section 117 provides for an application to be made for an order under s 116 by a highway or local authority on behalf of another person(for example an estate developer). The authority may however require such a person to make provision for their reasonable costs.

For the procedure as to s 116 notices, see Part I of Sched 12 to the Act. Section 316 provides that the procedure in the magistrates' court shall be by way of complaint for an order.

(c) Town and Country Planning Act 1971

By s 209(1) of the Act the Secretary of State may by order authorise the stopping up or diversion of any highway if he is satisfied that it is necessary in order to enable development to be carried out in accordance with planning permission or to be carried out by a government department. Section 209(3) provides that any such order may contain such incidental and consequential provisions as appear to the Secretary of State to be necessary or expedient, including provisions as to contributions to the cost of the work.

The procedure as to the making of an order by the Secretary of State is laid down by s 215, and where planning permission has not been granted, by s 216.

9 Root of the title

By s 23 of the Law of Property Act 1969 the period of commencement of title which a purchaser of unregistered land may require is now fifteen years instead of thirty years as originally specified in s 44(1) of the Law of Property Act 1925. In the case of registered land the vendor will be required to deduce title in accordance with s 110 of the Land Registration Act 1925. Further it should be noted that where unregistered building land is to be acquired with the benefit of easements (eg drainage and access) over adjoining land in the ownership of a third party, title to the easement will have to be investigated after exchange of contracts and accordingly the root of the title should be specified in the contract. The same considerations as to the deducing and investigation of title to easements apply in the case of registered land and an appropriate provision should be included in the contract. See also Chapter 4, head 7(*b*).

10 Other enquiries

Other matters which may be the subject of enquiries before contract in the case of an acquisition of land for building purposes are almost innumerable. Particular regard, though, may be had to rights of support, rights of light, overriding interests, problems of flooding, minerals and mining rights (other than coal: see Chapter 3, head 5), electricity and wayleave agreements, remedial costs in connection with disused tips and infrastructure costs.

Pre-contractual Searches

1 The Land Registry

A search of the index map and parcels index on form 96 (together with a plan for identification) will reveal if the land is registered and, if so, the title number. If the land is not registered the search will show whether the land is in an area of compulsory registration of title. The search will also show whether any applications of any sort are pending. Such a search should always be made prior to signature of the contract.

2 The Land Charges Register

There has been considerable debate as to whether a search should be made in the Land Charges Register against the vendor and his predecessors in title prior to the signature of the contract. Section 198(1) of the Law of Property Act 1925 provides that registration of any instrument or matter under the provisions of the Land Charges Act 1925, in any register kept at the Land Registry or elsewhere, shall be deemed to constitute actual notice of such instrument or matter and the fact of such registration, to all persons and for all purposes connected with the land affected as from the date of registration or other prescribed date and so long as the registration continues in force. However, s 24(1) of the Law of Property Act 1969 provides that where under a contract for the sale or other disposition of any estate or interest in land the title to which is *not* registered under the Land Registration Act 1925 any question arises whether the purchaser (which includes a lessee, mortgagee or other person acquiring or intending to acquire an estate or interest in the land, s 24(3)) had knowledge, at the time of entering into the contract, of a registered land charge, that question shall be determined by reference to his actual knowledge without regard to the provisions of s 198 of the Law of Property Act 1925. There is no definition in the 1969 Act of 'actual knowledge'.

However, s 24(4) provides that for the purposes of the section any knowledge acquired in the course of a transaction by a person who is acting therein as counsel, or as solicitor or other agent for another shall be treated as the knowledge of that other. It should be noted the position may also be affected by the conditions of sale, eg Condition 12(3) of the Law Society's General Conditions of Sale (1980 Ed).

The policy of the Law of Property Act 1969 suggests there is no necessity for purchasers to make a search in the Land Charges Register prior to signature of contract. However, such a search may reveal useful information as, for example, whether the vendor is a bankrupt which could save time at a later date. Further it is submitted that where there is a lengthy delay in completion, as in the case of a conditional contract or option agreement, a land charges search should always be made against the vendor and all estate owners subsequent to the root of title if the vendor's solicitor is prepared to reveal this latter information. Registration of the relevant contract will then have to be effected within the period of protection given by the search so as to ensure priority. If necessary such contemplated charge can be registered pursuant to a priority notice (Land Charges Act 1972, s 11). Section 24(3) specifically does *not* absolve a purchaser from making a search in the register of Local Land Charges. For provisions purporting to exclude s 24, see subs (2).

3 Local land charges

(a) General

A pre contract search must always be made in the local land charges register. It should always be remembered that the standard forms of search are not comprehensive and it is quite permissible to raise additional enquiries of a local authority. Apart from the multiplicity of general provisions which can arise there are a number of specific matters which can prohibit or partially restrict the development of a building estate. Such matters will need to be resolved before contracts can be exchanged. The items discussed below are not, however, comprehensive as each transaction will depend on its own particular circumstances.

(b) Tree preservation orders

By s 60(1), (1A) of the Town and County Planning Act 1971, as amended by Sched 15 of the Local Government, Planning and Land Act 1980, the local planning authority may make a tree preservation order with respect to such trees, groups of trees or woodlands as appears expedient. Such an order may prohibit the cutting down, topping, lopping, uprooting, wilful damage or wilful destruction of trees except with the consent of the authority which may be given subject to conditions. The order may also require replanting. Such orders are registrable as local land charges. The procedure on making a tree preservation order is dealt with in the Town and Country Planning (Tree Preservation Order) Regulations 1969 (SI 1969 No 17) as amended by the Town and Country Planning (Tree Preservation Order) (Amendment) Regulations 1981 (SI 1981 No 14).

Prima facie tree preservation orders could cause problems for a builder but in practice this should not be the case. Regulation 4 states that an order shall be in the form (or substantially in the form) set out in the Schedule to the Regulations. The standard form itself provides that an order shall not apply so as to require the consent of the authority to the cutting down, uprooting, topping or lopping of a tree where this is immediately required for the purpose of carrying out development pursuant to an authorised planning permission (form of order: Sched 2 para 3(*c*)). The onus of proof is on the defendant to establish that he comes within the exemption (*Edgeborough Building Co* v *Woking UDC* (1966) 198 EG 581).

The penalties for contravention of a tree preservation order are dealt with by s 102 of the Town and Country Planning Act 1971 (as amended by s 10 of the Town and Country Amenities Act 1974). It is no defence to a prosecution that the accused was unaware of the tree preservation order (*Maidstone Borough Council* v *Mortimer* (1982) 43 P&CR 67, CA). In addition to the statutory penalties it was held in *A-G* v *Melville Construction Co Ltd* (1968) 112 SJ 725 that an injunction would be granted to restrain the felling of trees, the subject of a tree preservation order, before a prosecution as it would not be possible to remedy the damage after the prosecution. For the right of the local authority to initiate proceedings in their own name see *Kent County Council* v *Batchelor* [1978] 3 All ER 980.

Possibly the best method of dealing with trees which are subject to a preservation order is to endeavour to fit them in the development by way of landscaping. To this end s 59(*a*) imposes a duty on the local planning authority to ensure, wherever it is appropriate, that in granting planning permission for any development adequate provision is made, by the imposition of conditions, for the preservation or planting of trees. For the special provisions relating to trees in conservation areas see s 61A added by s 8 of the Town and Country Amenities Act 1974 and also SI 1975 No 148. It should also be noted that if the Forestry Act 1967 applies a felling licence may be required from the Forestry Commissioners pursuant to s 9 of that Act.

(c) Listed buildings

By s 54(1) of the Town and Country Planning Act 1971, the Secretary of State is empowered to compile lists of buildings of special or architectural interest, or approve, with or without modifications, lists compiled by other persons or bodies of persons. The list is registrable as a local land charge (s 54(6)). However for the issue of a certificate by the Secretary of State that a building is not intended to be listed, see s 54A inserted by para 5 of Sched 15 to the Local Government, Planning and Land Act 1980 ('the 1980 Act'). By s 55(1) it is an offence to demolish or alter a listed building unless authorised pursuant to the Act. Section 55(2) provides that works for the demolition of a listed building or extension or alteration are authorised only if: (*a*) the local planning authority or the Secretary of State has granted a 'listed building consent' and the works are executed in accordance with the consent and any conditions; and (*b*) in the case of demolition, notice of the proposal has been given to the Royal Commission (as defined by s 55(3)) and thereafter either for a period of at least one month following the grant of the listed building consent, and before the commencement of the works, reasonable access to the building has been made available to members or officers of the Commission for the purpose of recording it; or the Commission has stated in writing that they have completed their recording of the building or that they do not wish to record it. As to the imposition of conditions see s 56(4), (5) as amended by paras 9 and 10 of Sched 15 to the 1980 Act. For the limit of duration of a listed building consent, see s 56A of the 1971 Act inserted by para 11 of Sched 15 to the 1980 Act. By s 56(2) certain planning consents granted prior to 1980 also operate as listed building consents, but this practice has now ceased to have effect (para 7 of Sched 15 to the 1980 Act).

Penalties for infringement of the section are set out in s 55(5). In addition the local planning authority may serve a 'listed building enforcement notice'; the procedure including appeals is set out in ss 96–100 of the 1971 Act as amended by para 17 of Sched 15 to the 1980 Act and para 9 of the Schedule to the Local Government Planning (Amendment) Act 1981. An application for consent to retain unauthorised works may now be made under s 55 (2A), (3A) of the 1971 Act, introduced by para 6 of Sched 15 to the 1980 Act. Section 55(6) provides a defence to a prosecution where it is proved that the works were urgently necessary in the interests of safety or health, or for the preservation of the building, and that notice in writing was given to the local planning authority as soon as reasonably practicable. Section 56(6) and Pt I of Sched 11 to the 1971

Act deal with the procedure for application for a listed building consent and any subsequent appeal. See also the Town and Country Planning (Listed Buildings and Buildings in Conservation Areas) Regulations 1977 (SI 1977 No 228). Part II of Sched 11 to the 1971 Act deals with the revocation of listed building consent. For compensation payable see ss 171–3 and 190; and for the imposition of 'a building preservation notice' where a building is not listed see s 58.

(d) Public footpaths and bridleways

General. The revelation by the local search of a public footpath or bridleway would at first sight seem to be relatively harmless. However, the public have become increasingly conscious of any attacks on the environment and numerous societies have been formed with the object of protecting public footpaths and bridleways. Such societies may vigorously oppose any application to divert or stop up a public footpath which is affected by proposed building development. For an example of residential development being commenced over the line of an existing footpath prior to a diversion order being made see *Ashby* v *Secretary of State for the Environment and Another* [1980] 1 All ER 508, CA. Such public footpaths and bridleways may be stopped up or diverted under the Town and Country Planning Act 1971 or the Highways Act 1980. It will depend on the circumstances of each case as to which of the two procedures is adopted. The Planning Act does, however, envisage development taking place as the result of a planning permission, whereas the grounds under the Highways Act makes no such provision.

The Town and Country Planning Act 1971. By s 210(1) of the Town and Country Planning Act 1971 subject to s 217 of the Act (which contains provisions as to the confirmation of orders) a competent authority may by order authorise the stopping up or diversion of a public footpath or bridleway if they are satisfied it is necessary to do so in order to enable development to be carried out in accordance with a planning permission, or to be carried out by a government department. By s 217 an order made under s 210 shall not take effect unless confirmed by the Secretary of State, or unless confirmed as an unopposed order by the authority who made it. The procedure is set out in Sched 20 of the Act, as amended by Sched 16 to the Wildlife and Countryside Act 1981. Paragraph 2 of Sched 20 provides that if there are no objections the authority may make the order without reference to the Secretary of State and themselves confirm the order. In the case of objections the Secretary of State will cause a local inquiry to be held (para 3). Such inquiry will inevitably cause delay and the builder client should be advised accordingly.

The Highways Act 1980. By s 119(1) of the Highways Act 1980, as amended by Sched 16 to the Wildlife and Countryside Act 1981, where it appears to a council as respects a footpath or bridleway (other than one that is a trunk road or a special road) that in the interests of the owner, lessee or occupier of land crossed by the path or way or of the public, it is expedient that the line of the path or way, or part of the line, should be diverted (whether on the land of the same or another owner) the council may make 'a public path diversion order'. Such order will be subject to confirmation by the appropriate minister or confirmed as an unopposed order. Secondly by s 118(1) of the Highways Act 1980 public footpaths and bridle-ways may be stopped up on the grounds that they are not needed for public use by means of a 'public path extinguishment order'. The order will require the confirmation of the Secretary of State unless unopposed. Compensation may be payable, see s 121(2). For procedure see ss 118(4) and 119(8) and Sched 6 to the 1980 Act (as amended by Sched 16 to the Wildlife and Countryside Act 1981).

(e) The Pipelines Act 1962

The replies to a local search will reveal whether a map has been deposited with the local authority pursuant to s 35 of the Pipelines Act 1962. If so it is prudent to inspect such a map to find out if the land is affected by pipes as defined by the Act. The plans are open to inspection free of charge at the local land charges office at all reasonable hours (s 35(5)). Seemingly rights of the owners are ease-ments (*Re Salvin's Indenture* [1938] 2 All ER 498) and overriding interests. Section 3 of the Act sets out the circumstances where a pipe may be lawfully diverted.

(f) Building and improvement lines

By s 74(1) of the Highways Act 1980 a highway authority may prescribe, in relation to either one side or both sides of a public highway, a frontage line for building. The prescription of such a building line is registrable as a local land charge and may, depend-ing on the circumstances, hinder or prevent residential develop-ment, particularly as a local planning authority is entitled to refuse planning permission for the development on the grounds there is a proposal for a building line (*Westminster Bank* v *Beverley Borough Council* [1971] AC 508). Where a building line is in force, no new buildings other than a boundary wall or fence can be erected, and no permanent excavation below the level of the highway can be made, nearer to the centre line of the highway than the building line, except with the consent of the relevant highway authority who can attach such time limit and conditions as they deem expedient (s 74(2)). A condition imposed in connection with the giving of a consent is binding on the successors in title to the land (s 74(4)). The penalties for contravention of the section are laid down by s 74(5). By s 74(6) a highway authority may revoke the whole or part of a building line where it is no longer necessary or desirable. The procedure in regard to both prescription and revocation is dealt with by Sched 9 to the Act. There is a right to compensation for any person whose property is injuriously affected by the prescribing of a building line, see s 74(8), (9). Similar restrictive provisions in regard to improvement lines are dealt with by s 73 of the Highways Act 1980.

4 Register of common land

In *G & K Ladenbau (UK) Ltd* v *Crawley and de Reya* [1978] 1 All ER 682 the purchaser's solicitors had enquired of the vendor's solicitors as to whether the property was subject to rights of common land and had received a negative reply but had failed to make a search in the register. Later it was found that there was an entry relating to part of the land, and it was held that although the solicitors were not bound to search the register in every case, the purchaser's solicitors had, on the facts, been negligent. Therefore with building land a search should always be made in the register of common land to ascertain the position under the Commons Registration Act 1965 where the land to be acquired has never been built on.

5 Coal mining

When acquiring land for building in areas which are subject to coal mining activities, it is essential to find out if such land is or will be affected by the future activities of the National Coal Board in which all coal and coal mines are now vested. Coal mining may render a site unfit for development or require special foundations to be constructed. The National Coal Board has statutory rights to withdraw support from the surface pursuant to ss 2 and 3 of and Sched 1 to the Coal Industry Act 1975. There is a right to inspect the coal working plans at the National Coal Board and to obtain copies pursuant to s 52 of the Coal Industry Nationalisation Act 1946. Application for information is made to the area surveyor and minerals manager at the National Coal Board Area Office in which the land is situate.

Chapter 4

Disposal of Building Estates

1 Freehold or leasehold

The builder client should be consulted as to the method by which he wishes to dispose of the individual houses. Financial considerations will inevitably be uppermost in his mind and, apart from explaining the basic legal position, the solicitor's role is somewhat limited. Obviously, in the case of a lease a premium will be charged and a ground rent can be imposed. Furthermore it will be possible to sell ground rents and thereby raise capital when required. Positive covenants can be more readily enforceable when imposed in a lease and indeed disposal by way of lease may be more appropriate in the case of, for example flats (see Chapter 5, head 1). From the purchaser's point of view, however, a freehold will naturally prove more attractive. For example, he will be free to carry out extensions and alterations and to assign the property without interference from a ground landlord.

2 The estate plan

Where there is a conveyance of small divided parts of a large building or plot, as is the case in a building estate or flats, each part should be described with sufficient accuracy and the use of a small scale ordnance map is inappropriate (*Scarfe* v *Adams* [1981] 1 All ER 843, CA). Accordingly a qualified surveyor should be instructed to prepare a detailed estate plan in conjunction with the builder and care must be taken to ensure such plan is accurate and of an adequate size and scale. For the Land Registry practice in the case of registered land see Chapter 4, head 11(*b*)(i). An estate plan marked 'for the purposes of identification only' should be avoided. See further Chapter 2, head 2 and also *Spall* v *Owen* (1981) 44 P & CR 36 for the pitfalls of using such a plan in relation to building estates.

3 The deposit

With reference to deposits Lord Macnaghten in *Soper* v *Arnold* (1889) 14 App Cas 429 at p 435 made the following observations:

The deposit serves two purposes—if the purchase is carried out it goes against the purchase money—but its primary purpose is this, it is a guarantee that the purchaser means business.

A deposit may be payable to the vendor, or more usually a third party, as, for example, the vendor's solicitor. It is, however, essential to define the capacity in which such third party holds the deposit monies. A builder will generally require the use of the deposit as soon as contracts have been exchanged to improve his cash flow, particularly if a large number of new houses are being sold. He will, therefore, require the deposit to be held as *agent* so that he can obtain immediate use of the money; a deposit holder who is the agent of the vendor must pay the deposit monies to the vendor on demand (*Edgell* v *Day* (1865) LR 1 CP 80). Furthermore, the agent will not be liable if sued for the return of the deposit as his duty is to the vendor only (*Edgell* v *Day*). However, since bankruptcies and liquidations are fairly common in the building trade a purchaser will require the deposit to be held by a third party as *stakeholder* since the deposit monies will not be able to be released without the consent of both parties (*Smith* v *Jackson* (1816) 1 Madd 618).

4 Rentcharges

The position in relation to the reservation of rentcharges has been radically altered by the Rentcharges Act 1977. Section 1 defines a rentcharge as any annual or other periodic sum charged on or issuing out of land, except (*a*) rent reserved by a lease or tenancy, or (*b*) any sum payable by way of interest. Section 2(1) provides that no rentcharge may be created, whether at law or in equity, after the coming into force of the section, ie 22 August 1977. Section 2(2) states that any instrument made after this date is void, to the extent that it purports to create a rentcharge.

Section 2(3) sets out certain exceptions to the general rule which includes the creation of an estate rentcharge. Section 2(4) defines 'an estate rentcharge' as a rentcharge created for the purpose: (*a*) of making covenants to be performed by the owner of the land affected by the rentcharge enforceable by the rent owner against the owner for the time being of the land; or (*b*) of meeting, or contributing towards the cost of the performance by the rent owner of covenants for the provision of services, the carrying out of maintenance or repairs, the effecting of insurance or the making of any payment by him for the benefit of the land affected by the rentcharge or for the benefit of that and other land. The definition envisages two types of rentcharge. Firstly a rentcharge designed to secure the enforcement of positive covenants by the rent owner. Secondly to provide for a service charge. By s 2(5) a rentcharge of more than a nominal amount shall not be treated as an estate rentcharge unless it represents a reasonable payment for the performance by the rent owner of any such covenant as is mentioned in subs (4)(*b*). Clearly the subsection will have considerable practical effects not only in relation to the sale of freehold flats, but also building estates generally.

5 Variable ground rents

In order to gain a continuing income from a newly erected property a developer may wish to impose a ground rent when leasing the dwelling. Over the years such ground rent may become virtually worthless as a result of inflation. Builders may therefore require provision to be made for ground rents to be reviewed during the term of the lease, as for example by reference to the Index of Retail Prices, at specified intervals or automatically on assignment of the lease, in accordance with an agreed formula based on the premium achieved on the assignment. In such circumstances, however, the rent on a future review may exceed two thirds of the rateable value of the premises on 'the appropriate day' (see ss 5 and 25(3) of the Rent Act 1977) whereby the lease would then become a protected tenancy within the Rent Act 1977 making it unlawful to require a premium on the assignment (s 120 of the Rent Act 1977) and thus rendering a mortgage unobtainable and the property unmarketable. For premiums allowable by statute in relation to certain long tenancies subject to rent increases which would otherwise be protected, see the provisions of s 127 of the Rent Act 1977 as amended by s 78 of the Housing Act 1980, and for a precedent incorporating these statutory provisions see *The Encyclopaedia of Forms and Precedents*, 4th Ed, service volume, additional forms, p 191 [62], form 79. However, for the possible risks considered to be involved in granting long leases at escalating rents, see *Emmet on Title*, 18th Ed, p. 756.

6 Building leases and building agreements

(a) General

In the case of a leasehold disposal the owner of land should be consulted as to which of the two methods of disposal by way of lease of land for building purposes he wishes to adopt. First, there is the possibility of a building lease, whereby an immediate lease is granted and the builder enters into a covenant to build. A premium or ground rent, or both, will be reserved out of such lease. If a satisfactory premium is obtained the landowner will have received his money and the builder will have an immediate interest in land which he can charge to raise money for building or otherwise dispose of. Thus both parties will probably have concluded a satisfactory bargain.

Alternatively, an agreement for lease can be entered into whereby the lease is granted only when the house or houses have been completed to the satisfaction of the grantor. In such cases the grantor will not receive the premium or rent until the lease is granted and the builder will have no permanent interest in the land until the lease is granted, being meanwhile a tenant at will or licensee. The agreement may contain an express provision against charging, and, in any event, it is a less valuable security than the lease itself. For example, by s 1(1) of the Building Societies Act 1962 a building society can only make an advance on the security of freehold or leasehold land.

A builder who is the owner of the land may himself enter into a building agreement with a purchaser for the construction of a dwellinghouse.

(b) Building leases between landowner and builder

Section 205(1) (iii) of the Law of Property Act 1925 defines 'a building lease' as a lease for building purposes or connected purposes. 'Building purposes' include the erecting and improving of and the adding to and the repairing of buildings. Thus the statutory definition extends to additions and improvements to buildings and is wider than the normal case where a builder constructs new houses. A covenant will require the developer tenant to complete the development to the satisfaction of the landlord's surveyor in accordance with plans and specifications attached to the lease, within a *specified period* of time. It is also advisable for the covenant to provide that the builder shall commence work forthwith. The builder will require a proviso to be added to the covenant to the effect that the building period will be extended in the event of delay arising as a result of events beyond his control. If the lease reserves a ground rent it is not implied that the land is to be built upon (*Wesley* v *Walker* (1878) 38 LT 284). Among the covenants which may be imposed are those limiting the number of dwellings, creating obligations to construct roads and sewers and to provide landscaping.

Section 19(1)(*b*) of the Landlord and Tenant Act 1927 provides that if a building lease is for more than forty years, and the lessor is not a government department or local or public authority, or a statutory or public utility company, the lease is deemed to be subject to the proviso that in the case of any assignment, underletting, charging or parting with possession (whether by the holders of the lease or any undertenant whether immediate or not) effected more than seven years before the end of the term no consent or licence shall be required, if notice in writing of the transaction is given to the lessor within six months after the transaction is effected.

The tenant should investigate the landlord's freehold title so as to avoid difficulties at a later stage if either an underlessee or a mortgagee requires the title to be deduced. Furthermore, in the case of registered land it may then be possible to obtain absolute as opposed to good leasehold title.

(c) Building agreements for lease between landowner and builder

The developer will enter into an agreement with the landowner to work to agreed plans and specifications within a specified time, and a lease or leases will be granted only on completion of the building to the satisfaction of the landowner or his architects. The developer will be allowed into possession of the site as a tenant at will or a licensee. In the case of a licence there will be an express provision that no lease will be created. The builder will require provisos that the building period will be extended if delay arises as a result of events beyond his control. Provision will also be made for re-entry on the land by the landowner in the case of breach of any covenant in the building agreement. To avoid doubt and uncertainty at a later date the form of the lease to be granted should be annexed to the agreement. When the work has been completed in accordance with the agreement the builder will hold the land on the terms of the lease as opposed to the building agreement (*Lowther* v *Heaver* (1889) 41 Ch D 248, CA). Similarly if the builder is entitled to have separate leases granted on completion of individual houses he holds each house when completed as though the lease had been granted (*Lowther* v *Heaver*). This rule applies even if the agreement provides that it shall not operate as a lease (*Strong* v *Stringer* (1889) 61 LT 470).

The agreement may contain a warranty that the grantor has a good and marketable title to grant the lease. Nevertheless it is prudent to investigate the freehold title so as to avoid difficulties at a later stage if either an underlessee or a mortgagee require the freehold title to be deduced. Furthermore, in the case of registered land it may then be possible to obtain absolute as opposed to good leasehold title when the lease is ultimately granted pursuant to the agreement. In the absence of express stipulation, however, the intending lessee is not entitled to insist on the freehold title being deduced (s 44(2) of the Law of Property Act 1925).

(d) Building agreements between builder and purchaser

As an alternative to a building agreement for lease it is possible to have a building agreement whereby the individual freehold plots of land are conveyed to the purchasers and the builder then undertakes to construct the dwellinghouse or houses in accordance with agreed plans and specifications. Alternatively the builder may agree to construct the house and the conveyance of the land and buildings to the purchasers will take place when the building has been constructed. Such arrangements can also be tailored to dispose of the property by way of lease. As to the most advantageous method to adopt from a stamp duty standpoint see the next section. As to the implied warranties in agreements of this nature see Chapter 9, head 2 (*b*).

(e) Stamp duty on building agreements

In the case of building agreements, difficulties arise as to whether the stamp duty is payable on the consideration for land alone or the land together with the buildings. The Inland Revenue have issued a statement which although not binding in law is helpful in practice. The statement is as follows:

(i) Subject to what is said under paragraph (iv) below, if under the contract for the sale or lease the purchaser or lessee is entitled to a conveyance or lease of the land in consideration only of the purchase price or rent of the site, the *ad valorem* duty on the conveyance or lease will be determined only by the amount of the purchase price or rent, although it may have been agreed that a house is to be built on the site at the expense of the purchaser or lessee. In such a case, the concurrent existence of a contract with the vendor or lessor or with any other person for the building of a house on the site will not increase the stamp duty chargeable on the conveyance or lease.

(ii) If under the contract the purchaser or lessee is not entitled to a conveyance or lease until a house has been built on the site at his expense and if the house is to be built by the vendor or lessor or by his agent or nominee, the payment of the building price by the purchaser or lessee will be part of the consideration for the conveyance or lease and will be liable to *ad valorem* duty accordingly.

(iii) When the position is as in paragraph (ii) above, and a purchaser or lessee not entitled to a conveyance or lease until a house has been erected at his expense in fact obtains a conveyance or lease when the house has been only partly erected, *ad valorem* duty is payable on the conveyance or lease on the proportionate amount of the building price attributable to the partial erection of the house as computed at the date of the conveyance or lease.

(iv) (*a*) If at the date of the contract a house has been wholly or partly erected by the vendor or lessor or by his agent or nominee or by a builder not employed by the purchaser or lessee, it normally forms part of the subject matter of the sale or lease and the consideration or apportioned consideration for that building (as existing at the date of the contract) is accordingly liable to *ad valorem* duty.

(*b*) If, at the date of the contract, a house has been wholly or partly erected by the purchaser or lessee or by any person on his behalf the consideration or apportioned consideration for the house wholly or partly erected will not normally form part of the consideration for the sale or lease and accordingly will not be liable to *ad valorem* duty.

(*c*) This paragraph is subject to what is said in paragraphs (ii) and (iii) above.

(v) The contract referred to above may be contained in more than one instrument or it may be partly written and partly verbal. It includes any contractual arrangements between the parties.

These observations do not have the force of law and are given by the Inland Revenue merely with the object of assisting the taxpayer. The Board are not bound by them and the circumstances of any particular case may call for special consideration. Therefore in cases of doubt the documentation should be submitted for adjudication of the duty chargeable.

7 Easements

(a) The perpetuity rule

There will be granted to the purchaser and his successors in title, in common with the owners and occupiers of other land comprised in the building estate, appropriate rights to use the roads, drains, sewers, and other services serving the building estate. Conversely, there will be excepted and reserved to the vendor and the owners and occupiers of all other lands comprised in the building estate the right to use in common with the purchaser the roads, drains, sewers, and other services on or under the land conveyed to him.

When drafting or approving such easements care must be taken not to offend the rule against perpetuities. This is particularly so when such roads and sewers have not yet been constructed but are to be put in at an uncertain future date. Section 162(1)(*d*)(iv) of the Law of Property Act 1925 provides that, for the avoidance of doubt, the rule against perpetuities does not and shall be deemed never to have applied to any grant, exception, or reservation of any right of entry on, or user of, the surface of land or of any easements,

rights or privileges over or under land for the purposes of constructing, laying down, altering, repairing, renewing, cleansing and maintaining sewers, watercourses, cesspools, gutters, drains, water pipes,
gas pipes, electric wires or cables or other like works. It was held
in *Dunn* v *Blackdown Properties Ltd* [1961] Ch 433 that the section
applied only to ancillary rights and did not validate a right which
was to arise at some uncertain date in the future. The clauses
granting or reserving future easements should therefore provide that
the perpetuity period applicable will be eighty years: a provision to
this effect will not offend the perpetuity rule (see s 1(1) of the
Perpetuities and Accumulations Act 1964). However, it would seem
that even if the right is not to be exercised within the perpetuity
period it may be valid as regards roads, pipes etc constructed within
twenty-one years (ss 3 and 15(5) of the 1964 Act).

(b) Investigation of title to an easement

When acting for the purchaser in the case of non-registered land
it is essential to confirm that the vendor has a good and marketable
title to grant an easement over, for example, the estate road. It may
be that the whole of the building estate is comprised in the same
title as the property conveyed: in such circumstances no difficulty
will arise. However, the rights which are to be granted may pass
over or under land which is comprised in several titles and it will
then be necessary to investigate each of the titles in question.

The same problem arises in the case of registered land. A purchaser's solicitor may accept a certificate of official inspection of the
filed plan instead of a copy of the actual filed plan. Such a certificate
will not show the extent of the land in the ownership of the vendor
and, accordingly, it will not be possible to confirm that such vendor
is validly entitled to grant the easements in question. The vendor's
solicitors should therefore request the registry when granting the
letter approving the standard form of draft transfer to confirm that
easements granted in the standard form set out in the transfer will
be registered as appurtenant to the purchaser's title. A copy of such
letter can then be produced to each individual purchaser.

When this procedure is not followed the purchaser should obtain
an office copy of the filed plan to satisfy himself as to easements.
Alternatively, the registry can be asked when application is made
for a certificate of inspection of the filed plan to confirm that the
specific rights are within the title of the vendor. The vendor's
solicitor may request that this procedure is adopted on the issue of
all certificates of official inspection of the filed plan. See also *Registered Land Practice Notes*, 1982/83, B7: proof of easements.

8 Building schemes

(a) Requirements

To ensure that not only subsequent owners of the land but also the various house owners on the building estate can enforce restrictive covenants imposed on the estate amongst themselves it is necessary to establish 'a building scheme'. In *Elliston* v *Reacher* [1908] 2 Ch 665 certain useful guidelines were laid down as to the elements of a building scheme which are as follows:

(i) The various house owners derive title from a common vendor;

(ii) The vendor has, prior to the sale to the various house owners, laid out a building estate, or a defined portion, for sale in lots subject to restrictions intended to be imposed on all lots, and which, though varying in details as to particular lots, are consistent only with some general scheme or development. The area over which the scheme is to operate must be clearly defined (*Read* v *Bickerstaff* [1909] 2 Ch 305);

(iii) The common vendor intends such restrictions to be for the benefit of all the lots intended to be sold, whether or not they were also intended to be and were for the benefit of other land retained by the vendor; and

(iv) Both the plaintiffs and the defendants, or their predecessors in title, purchased their lots from the common vendor on the footing that the restrictions, subject to which the purchases were made, were to enure for the benefit of the other lots included in the general scheme, whether or not they were also to enure for the benefit of other lands retained by the vendor.

Such a scheme may be supported by a deed of mutual covenant as in *Baxter* v *Four Oaks Properties Ltd* [1965] Ch 816 where it was held there was a building scheme even though the property had not previously been laid out in plots. It is usual for the vendor to reserve the right to vary or release the covenants and this will not necessarily invalidate a building scheme (*Eagling* v *Gardner* [1970] 2 All ER 838). It is also possible to create a subsidiary building scheme in addition to the principal scheme (see *Lawrence* v *South County Freeholds Ltd* [1939] Ch 656). A scheme can be terminated by all the purchasers mutually agreeing to release themselves (*Re Pinewood Estate, Farnborough, New Ideal Homestead Ltd* v *Levack* [1958] Ch 280). For a precedent imposing a building scheme, see *The Encyclopaedia of Forms and Precedents*, 4th Ed, vol 18, p 697.

(b) Registration of restrictive covenants

In the case of unregistered land the vendor should register at the Land Charges Register any restrictive covenant imposed under a building scheme as a class D(ii) entry (see s 2(5) of the Land Charges Act 1972) so that there is no danger of such covenants being rendered void against a subsequent purchaser for value of the legal estate. In the case of a larger estate, however, it is quite possible that as a result of oversight the vendor will fail to register some of the covenants. The question arises as to whether a purchaser for value of the legal estate will take free from such covenants. It has been argued that as a building scheme gives rise to reciprocity of obligations between the purchasers there is nothing to register and the obligations are not void for want of registration. For further detailed discussion on this topic see *Emmet on Title* 18th Ed, p 552. As a precautionary measure when acting for the purchaser of a new house on a building estate subject to a building scheme the solicitor can request written confirmation that all covenants have been registered on previous sales off and will be so registered in the case of future sales off. As regards registered land, there is no requirement in the Land Registration Act 1925 or the rules to enter notice of a building scheme. However, if, in practice, the elements of a building scheme are established to the satisfaction of the registrar reference to such a scheme will be made when entering notice on the register of the covenants made pursuant to such scheme.

9 Positive covenants

(a) Definition

A positive covenant is one which requires the covenantor to expend money or carry out some positive act as, for example, to pay for or construct the roads on a building estate. Each covenant is a matter for individual interpretation but the court will not construe a covenant which is restrictive in form but positive in effect as a restrictive covenant. Conversely, if a covenant is positive in terms but restrictive in effect it will be construed as a restrictive covenant (*Clegg* v *Hands* (1890) 44 Ch D 503).

(b) The burden

The burden of a positive covenant (except in the case of a leasehold) does not as a rule run with the land (*Austerberry* v *Oldham Corporation* (1885) 29 Ch D 750). The question arises as to how in the case of freeholds a positive covenant can be imposed and enforced against subsequent owners of the land. Some help is given by the case of *Halsall* v *Brizell* [1957] Ch 169 where on the sale of land as building plots the vendors retained the roads and sewers together with a promenade along a sea wall. A deed of covenant was entered into whereby the purchasers of the plots covenanted for themselves, their heirs, executors, administrators and assigns with the vendors, their heirs and assigns so far as related to their plots that they would contribute and pay a fair proportion of maintaining the roads on the estate, the sea wall, promenade, and also drains and sewers. A subsequent purchaser acquired one of the plots with the dwellinghouse erected on it and the property was conveyed to him subject to the covenant contained in the deed of covenant and he then refused to pay a fair proportion of the maintenance costs. It was held the purchaser's executors were bound to accept the burden of the covenant for contribution as they desired to take its benefits, eg to use the roads leading to their house and to have the use of the sewers which were vested in the plaintiffs. Thus the positive covenants were enforceable against successors in title.

If it is desired to impose positive covenants which are enforceable against successors in title, it is submitted that the more appropriate vehicle for disposal of the land is probably a lease rather than a conveyance of the freehold. However, consideration should also be given to the effect of s 2(4)(*a*) of the Rentcharges Act 1977 and the possibility of imposing an estate rentcharge in the case of freeholds so as to secure the enforcement of positive covenants: see Chapter 4, head 4.

(c) Registered land

In the case of registered land the mere fact that a positive covenant has been noted on the register will not make it binding on a subsequent purchaser (*Cator* v *Newton and Bates* [1940] 1 KB 415 and s 52(2) of the Land Registration Act 1925).

10 Non-registered land—general note

In the case of the disposal of dwellings where the land is not registered the usual conveyancing formalities will have to be complied with. However, assuming that the title to the whole estate is the same there will inevitably be a great deal of repetitive work. It is therefore essential to set up a system with the client so that the formalities are reduced to a minimum and the transaction completed as quickly as possible. A detailed instruction sheet can be agreed with the builder; this can then be completed and sent to the solicitor with an appropriate plan as soon as a prospective purchaser has been found. It will also be necessary for the solicitor to prepare standard forms of replies to enquiries before contract, draft contracts, and conveyances together with a standard form of letter which can be sent off to the other solicitors at the outset of the transaction thus giving them as much information as possible. The vendor's solicitor may, however, find it desirable to effect voluntary registration of title to the building estate (see below).

11 Registered land

(a) Voluntary registration of title

As a general rule since January 1967 there has been no voluntary registration of title of land outside an area of compulsory registration. Building estates are, however, an exception to the rule. Subject to certain conditions being satisfied and undertakings being given, the registry will accept voluntary first registration of title of a building estate. Details of the procedure are set out in Land Registry's Practice Leaflet for Solicitors No 12 (April 1981 Ed). Applications for voluntary registration of development plots, or purpose built flat developments of comparable size, will be accepted on the conditions set out below. There should be lodged with the application for first registration certificates and undertakings given by the person or company applying for first registration, or by his or their solicitors (or partly by the solicitors and partly by the client) as follows:

(i) A certificate that the freehold/leasehold estate to be registered, when developed, will comprise not less than twenty house plots or a like number of units in a purpose-built flat development or maisonette development, exclusive of garages and other outbuildings.

(ii) A certificate that the applicant has obtained, or is satisfied that he will obtain, outline planning permission for the whole of the land sought to be registered and that he will go on to seek detailed planning permission.

(iii) A certificate that the applicant intends, within two years from the date of the application for first registration, to begin selling freehold plots, houses, flats or maisonettes to individual purchasers, or granting leases thereof for terms of ninety years or more.

(iv) An undertaking (if a survey of the boundaries is found to be essential before the official plan of the title can be prepared for first registration) to pay the requisite survey fee.

(v) An undertaking that the applicant will submit to the Land Registry two copies of the layout plan of the estate for official approval as soon as possible, and well before the first transfer or lease is likely to be lodged for registration. The applicant understands that, once the plan has been officially approved, it may be used by the solicitors acting for purchasers or lessees for the purpose of applying for official searches and inspections of the register of the parent title, and that extracts taken from it may also be used as plans for annexing to instruments of transfer or lease.

(vi) An undertaking that, in laying down the roads and erecting houses and boundary structures, there will be no departure from the proposals incorporated in the approved estate layout plan; but that, if it is necessary to make a change in the estate layout affecting the position or extent of any of the plots to be disposed of, the Land Registry will be informed of the decision immediately and well before any alteration is allowed to occur on the site; and a further undertaking that, at the same time, the previously approved estate plan will be returned to the Land Registry and the revised plan submitted in duplicate for approval. The applicant understands that he will then be responsible for taking all necessary steps for ensuring that the lodgment of all transfers or leases which might be affected by the change is suspended until a fresh layout plan has been prepared and officially approved.

(vii) An undertaking to submit to the Land Registry as soon as possible and before any transfer or lease on the estate is engrossed, two copies of the draft form of standard transfer or lease for official approval as to form; and a further undertaking that all transfers or leases to be used on the estate will be drawn in that standard form, allowing only for such variations as may be necessary for defining the dispositionary powers of joint purchasers or corporate purchasers, or for describing different kinds of rights (as, for example, rights of way over side or rear passageways) according to the character of the layout.

A form of certificate incorporating the above provisions (Form C 168) is shown in the appendix to the official leaflet. See also *The Encyclopaedia of Forms and Precedents*, 4th Ed, vol 17, p 318.

In the light of these provisions there must be close co-operation between the builder, his solicitor and surveyor and the Land Registry. In particular the Land Registry should be kept informed of any departure from the approved plan. Failure to observe the undertakings may result in the registrar refusing to effect registration of title until the appropriate breaches have been remedied.

Application for voluntary registration of title by local authorities and development corporations in respect of building land will be entertained if the applications contain a statement either:

(*a*) that the authority will sell the freehold of new dwellings, built or to be built, on the land sought to be registered to individual purchasers, or will grant leases of ninety years or more of those dwellings; or (*b*) that the authority will sell the land to developers who will thereafter sell or lease individual houses for like purposes.

(b) Registry practice with building estates

(i) *The estate layout plan.* In order that the sale of dwellings proceeds both smoothly and quickly it is necessary for both parties' solicitors to co-operate fully, not only between themselves but also with the Land Registry. The vendor's solicitor's activities in regard to such co-operation will be crucial. He is 'the link man' not only with the purchaser's solicitors but also with the builder and his other professional advisers.

The first step will be to lodge at the appropriate district registry for approval the estate layout plan in duplicate. One copy will be returned when approved. The estate layout plan must show clearly the boundary of the development; be drawn to a recognised and adequate scale; define clearly each plot and state the plot numbers; and show all estate roads. In short, the plan must be accurate and give the fullest details not only of the whole development but also the individual plots to be sold off. Plans 'for identification purposes only' are unacceptable to the registry. See also *Registered Land Practice Notes*, 1982/83, C1: Requirements for plans in dispositions of registered land. In cases of doubt it will be prudent to seek the advice or guidance of the registry. For further detailed guidance see HM Land Registry Practice Leaflet No 7, entitled 'Development of Registered Building Estates'. The leaflet deals not only with the estate layout plan but also building estates generally and the practitioner will find it most useful to have a copy available from the outset. The leaflet can be obtained free of charge from any district land registry. See also *Registered Land Practice Notes*, 1982/83, Section B for further guidance on Land Registry Practice in regard to Registered Building Developments.

Problems will almost inevitably arise, in practice, because of alterations made to the estate layout by the builder. If care is not taken such variations will be carried out without the vendor's solicitor's knowledge and will therefore not be communicated to the registry. At the outset of the development it is therefore essential for the builder's solicitors to inform the client, and also the other professional advisers involved, of the difficulties that can arise in the event of an unapproved deviation from the estate layout plan. Extra care at this stage can save time later. This is particularly so as the registry will from time to time carry out surveys of the estate and unapproved variations will then become apparent.

A plan must also be attached to each individual transfer on the sale off of a plot on the estate. Preferably to avoid doubt the transfer plan should be the approved layout plan with the plot itself clearly marked. If, however, an extract from the site layout plan is used, sufficient detail must be given for the registry to relate the plot sold off to the appropriate layout plan.

(ii) Deposit of certificate. In the case of larger building estates which will be developed over a long period the vendor's or landlord's land or charge certificate may be deposited at the registry and will then be allocated a deposit number. Reference to the deposit number will be made by the purchaser when effecting registration of the transfer. The vendor's solicitors can obtain appropriate numbers of office copy entries and copies of the filed plan, from time to time, as required. The application to the registry for office copy entries is made on form A44.

(iii) Certification of the filed plan. The purchaser will receive office copy entries from the vendor or alternatively will be supplied with an authority to inspect the register which will enable him to obtain office copy entries for himself on application being made on form A44. If the filed plan is bulky and difficult to reproduce it may be impractical to supply a copy. Nevertheless, the purchaser will require to satisfy himself that the plot purchased is within the vendor's title and to discover whether any references as regards colour or otherwise shown on the filed plan and referred to in the office copy entries of the register affect the plot in question.

Accordingly, a procedure has been evolved which considerably simplifies the matter in practice. An application in form 101 is made to the registry for a certificate of inspection of the filed plan. A certificate to that effect will be given by the registry in form 102 certifying that the plot is within the vendor's title, and is not affected by any colour or other reference shown on the filed plan and mentioned in the entries on the register. Alternatively, details of how the plot is affected will be revealed. No priority is conferred by the certificate but its accuracy is guaranteed and the purchaser will, therefore, have an indemnity against any loss incurred as a result of an error in the certificates: see s 83(3) of the Land Registration Act 1925.

(iv) The official search. Immediately prior to completion the purchaser must make an official search of the register on form 94. Where an estate layout plan has been lodged the search will make reference to the appropriate plot number. No fee is payable. The certificate of the result of the search will reveal whether there have been any adverse entries on the register since the date of the office copy entries, and confirm the plot is within the vendor's registered title. The purchaser has thirty working days' priority within which

to effect registration: the date of the expiration of the priority will be endorsed on the result of the search.

(c) The 'title shown' procedure

(i) *General.* This exceptional procedure is designed to save time and expense for both the vendor's and the purchaser's solicitors in cases where building land with unregistered title is to be sold off and numerous subsequent transfers will then require registration. The registry will investigate the title to the land and when satisfied will issue 'a letter as to title' setting out the terms on which an absolute title will be granted to the individual purchasers. Thus it will not be necessary for the vendor's solicitor to deduce title in every case, nor for the purchaser's solicitor to investigate title. The procedure is particularly relevant where a builder sells the freehold reversion of a leasehold estate to the existing lessees. The procedure is only available with the fullest co-operation of the vendor's solicitors and where:

(a) the land is in an area of compulsory registration of title;
(b) the title to the whole of the estate is contained under a single conveyance, or, where there are several conveyances, there are no complexities in the title;
(c) the estate is a large one which will be disposed of easily;
(d) the topography of the land comprising the estate is straightforward and free from complexities;
(e) the registry require the fullest co-operation in the investigation of the estate owner's title from the solicitor concerned.

(ii) *Application for the procedure.* The procedure is outside the scope of the Land Registration Acts and Rules and there is no right to demand the use of the procedure which is entirely at the registrar's discretion. Application should be made to the registrar before negotiations are commenced for the disposal of the properties. Initially the vendor's solicitors will write to the registry setting out the circumstances as to why in their opinion the procedure is appropriate. This will be followed by an interview with the registrar to discuss the matter further. The decision can then be made as to whether the procedure should be adopted.

There should be lodged with the registry at the earliest opportunity the following documents:

(a) A plan (scale of not less than 1/2500) showing the area of land the subject of the application. The site layout plan may suffice.
(b A schedule in triplicate of the properties the subject of the application.

(*c*) A marked copy abstract of title. In practice, it may be advisable to lodge the original deeds and indeed the registry may insist that this be done.

(*d*) A standard form of draft conveyance to the individual purchasers.

The applicant will have to supply sufficient evidence to enable the registry to identify the property on the ordnance map. The registry will investigate the title. A statutory declaration will be required from the vendor or his solicitors confirming that the properties covered by the investigation are still in the ownership of the vendor and that no restrictive covenants have been imposed, or easements granted, on previous sales. There may be other matters requiring to be covered by the statutory declaration. The registry will advise as to the contents and also approve the form of statutory declaration.

(iii) The letter as to title. In the letter as to title the Chief Land Registrar states (inter alia) that he will register as absolute the title of any purchaser from the named vendor of any of the properties set out in the schedule to the letter. The purchaser will be required to produce to the registry the following:

(*a*) Form of application for first registration of title together with sufficient details to identify the property on the ordnance map.

(*b*) A conveyance in standard form approved by the registry together with a certified copy.

(*c*) Where a reversion is being sold, the counterpart lease.

(*d*) A clear search in HM Land Charges Register against the vendor.

(*e*) The appropriate fee.

If there are any variations in the title the registry must be informed immediately. For example, a change of trustee must be notified. Where the procedure is applicable the vendor's solicitor when preparing a draft contract for the sale of the plot will have to insert a special condition as to the vendor's title. The letter as to title and the standard form of conveyance can be incorporated in the draft contract so as to make the position clear.

Chapter 5

Flats

1 Method of disposal

A builder who acquires land with a view to developing a block of flats encounters rather more complex legal and technical problems than if he were dealing with dwellinghouses. Easements of access, shelter, support, running of water, soil, gas, electricity etc, will have to be reserved in favour of the various flat owners, and restrictive covenants as to user entered into. Furthermore, management schemes involving positive covenants, for example, repair and insurance, will have to be arranged to ensure that the flats and common parts of the block are properly managed and maintained. Sufficient funds will have to be made available by the flat owners to meet these expenses.

The choice of method of disposal of the flats is crucial if these problems are to be dealt with satisfactorily, and should be discussed with the developer at the earliest opportunity, if possible prior to the acquisition of the site. A method of disposal and a management scheme will have to be established to satisfy not only the individual purchasers but also their mortgagees. As a general rule, building societies will not lend money on the security of flats unless adequate provisions have been made for their management. In practice, this means loans will not be made on the security of a freehold flat. This attitude is adopted because of the difficulty of enforcing positive covenants in the case of freeholds. In the case of two freehold flats which will have few or no common amenities a freehold disposal by way of transfer or covenant may be acceptable. Otherwise, in the case of a larger development it is submitted that leases of the individual flats should be granted so that the burden of the positive covenants can be made to run with the land. Difficulties as regards the enforcement of the burden of positive covenants have been discussed at Chapter 4, head 9(*b*).

It should be noted, however, that schemes have also been devised whereby a freehold flat is transferred, and a rentcharge reserved: see also ss 2(3), (4) and (5) of the Rentcharges Act 1977. Leases, however, seem to have been more commonly adopted in practice. As to variable ground rents on the grant of the lease of a flat, see Chapter 4, head 5.

2 Management schemes

It is in the interests of the flat owners to see that there is in operation a satisfactory management scheme. The builder, however, will almost certainly wish to dissociate himself from the problems of administration as soon as the last property has been sold. A developer may administer the flats through his agents but this will involve extra expense which will ultimately devolve on the tenants, and the developer will remain liable as landlord.

Such managing agents must remain independent of the landlord: see *Finchbourne Ltd* v *Rodrigues* [1976] 3 All ER 581 where the firm of agents was wholly owned by the lessor. Furthermore where a dispute arises the court will not allow the landlord's managing agent and surveyor to decide arbitrarily the amount of the tenants' contribution and in such circumstances will require an independent surveyor to be appointed (*Concorde Graphics Ltd* v *Andromeda Investments SA* (1983) 265 EG 386). A scheme should be devised whereby the interests of the individual flat owners are protected while allowing the developer to retire from the scene at the earliest opportunity.

There are a number of schemes which have been used to deal with the problem. The flat owners may form a tenants' association to run the flats in conjunction with the developer/landlord. Such an arrangement has two disadvantages: firstly, the developer is still involved, although to a lesser degree than if formal management were undertaken; secondly, the association will have no legal standing and may well prove weak and ineffectual. The commonest and most effective solution is to form a management company, whereby the developer transfers the freehold reversion of the leases granted to a company, the shareholders of which are the flat owners themselves. Thus the developer drops out altogether and the flat owners own the freehold. The management company will administer the flats and arrange for the service charge to be collected. As the tenants themselves will be administering a management scheme of this type, the cost of employing outside agents will be avoided. Practical pitfalls can arise in that it may prove difficult to find flat owners who are willing to carry out the work of the management function, although this is not an insuperable hurdle. To avoid legal complications the management company can be unlimited, or perhaps preferably limited by guarantee, since an unlimited liability may be a deterrent to tenants becoming shareholders. Provisions as to membership of the management company will be written into the sale agreement of each individual flat.

3 Service charges

When in operation the most contentious part of management schemes can be the imposition of and the amount of the service charge. Two main difficulties arise: Firstly, is it in order to make a particular charge? Secondly, is such a charge excessive? In the lease the landlord will convenant to provide certain services. Conversely, the tenant will enter into a covenant to pay a proportionate part, relative to his particular flat, of the expenses incurred by the landlord in repairing, painting, maintaining, insuring, heating, lighting etc, the common parts of the building in which the flats are situate. In recent times, with the very high rate of inflation, the burden of such service charges has become considerable and may constitute a possible deterrent to a prospective purchaser of a flat. In preparing the tenant's service charge covenant the draftsman must, therefore, endeavour to prepare a clause which, so far as is possible, is fair to all parties while making readily available a fund to meet the expenses of management.

With regard to the proportion of service charge to be paid by each flat owner certainty is important so that there can be no debate between the flat owners once the management scheme has become operative. Some service charges are based on the ratio of the rateable value of the demised flat to the total rateable value of the building as a whole. Difficulties will immediately arise if the flat owner appeals against his rate assessment. A considerable time will elapse before such an appeal is resolved and meanwhile the service charge provision will probably prove inoperable. There may, in any case, be a delay in assessing the rateable value of the flats. Provision will therefore have to be made in the service charge clause to provide for these difficulties. Furthermore the rateable value once fixed can alter over a period of time. Accordingly the lease should provide whether the rateable value is that applicable at the date of the lease or the rateable value which may arise from time to time during the course of the term: see further *Moorcroft Estates Ltd* v *Doxford and Another* (1979) 254 EG 871.

The developer may impose an arbitrary fractional proportion, and assuming that the proportion is not unreasonable such a calculation will give less scope for dispute. Alternatively, a fairer formula is to relate the proportion of the service charge to the floor areas of each the flats: again there is less scope for dispute. Problems can, however, arise in both these cases where the bulk of the flats have been sold subject to the covenant but the later prospective purchasers jib at the proportion they are required to pay and claim it to be unfair.

From the purchaser's viewpoint the service charge clause should be carefully studied to ascertain the matters covered and the mechanics of its operation. In large blocks of flats, where machinery is involved, eg a lift, provision may be made for depreciation and this may cause a substantial increase in the service charge. The clause should provide for full and detailed audited accounts of the service charge cost to be produced to the tenant if required (*West Central Investments Ltd* v *Borovik* (1976) 241 EG 609). The landlord's statutory duties in regard to service charges are now set out in Sched 19 to the Housing Act 1980 which deals (inter alia) with service charge and relevant costs (para 1); limitation of service charges (paras 2–6); information as to relevant costs (para 7); information held by superior landlord (para 8); determination of reasonableness (paras 11–12); offences (para 13); exceptions (paras 14–15) and definitions (para 16). The landlord cannot impose an increased service charge contribution when, for example, excess heating costs arise as a result of additional premises being incorporated in the original building, and in such circumstances the court will do whatever is fair and reasonable (*Pole Properties Ltd* v *Feinberg* (1981) 259 EG 417). Where a landlord is under a statutory obligation to carry out repairs pursuant to the Housing Act 1961 the cost cannot be recouped from the tenant by way of a service charge (*Campden Hill Towers Ltd* v *Gardner* [1977] QB 823). Furthermore, a service charge clause cannot exclude the jurisdiction of the courts as to a question of law (*Re Davstone Estates Ltd's Leases* [1969] 2 Ch 378).

4 Registered land

Rule 54 of the Land Registration Rules 1925 provides that on the first registration of a proprietor of a flat a plan must be supplied of the surface over which the flat lies, together with notes of any rights of access, whether held in common with others or not, or obligations affecting other tenements for the benefit of the flat in question. The registrar may ask for a further description in addition to the plan supplied.

There is a proviso to the rule to the effect that a plan of the land in question will not be needed if sufficient reference is made to the general map, but, in practice, the registry will require a plan of the land to be deposited. (See also *Registered Land Practice Notes*, 1982/83, C2: Plans of flats.)

Chapter 6

Planning Applications and Inquiries

1 Formalities for application for planning permission

Section 25 of the Town and Country Planning Act 1971 requires any application to a local planning authority for planning permission to be made in such a manner as may be prescribed by the regulations under the Act and provides that it shall include such particulars, and be verified by such evidence, as may be required by the regulations or by directions given by the local planning authority. See art 5(1) of the Town and Country Planning General Development Order 1977 (SI 1977 No 289) (GDO 1977) as to applications for planning permission generally and art 5(2) for applications for 'outline permission'. Article 6(1) deals with applications for approval of reserved matters. As to the relationship between applications for outline planning permission and subsequent approval of reserved matters and in particular the right to make successive applications for approval of reserved matters, see *Heron Corporation* v *Manchester City Council* [1978] 1 WLR 937. Assuming the relevant formalities are observed a person other than the owner of the land may make an application for planning permission. Such a person will, however, be well advised to protect his interests by entering into an option or conditional contract with the vendor as outlined in Chapter 1.

From the point of view of any possible subsequent planning appeal it is important to comply with the relevant formalities and, in particular, the provisions of ss 26 and 27 of the Town and Country Planning Act 1971. Section 26 requires, in certain circumstances, publication of the notice of application and a certificate, to be lodged with the local planning authority, that the section has been complied with (see also art 8 of the GDO 1977). Section 27 requires a certificate to be lodged with the local planning authority as to notification of applications to owners and agricultural tenants (see also art 9 of the GDO 1977). If there is an appeal it is necessary to lodge with the notice of appeal a copy of the s 26 (if applicable) or s 27 certificate. Failure to comply with s 27 may not, necessarily, affect the jurisdiction of the minister to determine the appeal, (however see *R* v *Bradford-on-Avon UDC* [1964] 1 WLR 1136). Care at the application stage is, nevertheless, very important: see also *English* v *Dedham Vale Properties Ltd* [1978] 1 All ER 382.

2 Application fees

Section 87(1) of the Local Government, Planning and Land Act 1980 authorises the Secretary of State to make such regulations as he thinks fit for the payment of fees in relation to planning applications and deemed applications. The regulations at present applicable are the Town & Country Planning (Fees for Applications and Deemed Applications) Regulations 1981 (SI 1981 No 369) as amended by the Town and Country Planning (Fees for Applications and Deemed Applications) (Amendment) Regulations 1982 (SI 1982 No 716). In the case of a large development the fees can be substantial and details of such fees are set out in Sched 1 to the 1982 Regulations. For further guidance as to the operation of the Regulations, see Department of the Environment circular 14/82, 'Town and Country Planning (Fees for Applications and Deemed Applications) (Amendment) Regulations'.

3 Right to appeal

By s 36(1) (as amended by para 4(2) of Sched 15 to the Local Government, Planning and Land Act 1980) where an application for planning permission to develop land, or for any consent, agreement or approval required by a condition attached to a planning permission, or for any approval required under a development order is refused by a local planning authority or is granted subject to conditions, the applicant, if he is aggrieved by their decision, may by notice appeal to the Secretary of State. The notice must be lodged within six months of the notice of the decision or of the expiry of the appropriate period allowed under art 7(6) of the GDO 1977 as amended (see below), or such longer period as the Secretary of State may allow (art 20(1), (1A) of the GDO 1977). Note that it is the applicant for planning permission who has the right to appeal: *not* the owner of the land.

It must be borne in mind that when appealing against a limited consent, or conditions attached to a consent, s 36(3) empowers the Secretary of State to reverse or vary any part of the decision of the local planning authority, whether the appeal relates to that part or not, and may deal with the application as if it had been made to him in the first instance. It is therefore possible to make matters worse rather than better by appealing.

Section 37 (as amended by para 4(3) of Sched 15 to the 1980 Act) gives a right of appeal in the event of a 'deemed refusal' where the local planning authority has failed to give a decision within the period prescribed by the development order, or within such extended period as may have been agreed upon in writing. The right to appeal arises in the case of a deemed refusal if the authority fail to give a decision within eight weeks of the receipt of a valid application pursuant to s 36(1) (which includes payment of the appropriate fee) or at the expiration of such extended period as may be agreed in writing between the parties (art 7(6) of the GDO 1977 and arts 7 (6A), (6B) and (7A) of the Town and Country Planning General Development (Amendment) Order 1980 (SI 1980 No 1946)).

Section 35(1) provides that the Secretary of State may give directions requiring applications for planning permission to be referred to him instead of being dealt with by local planning authorities. The procedure for an inquiry in the case of a referred application is similar to an ordinary appeal inquiry.

4 Notice of appeal

On receipt of a planning refusal, or a consent subject to unsatisfactory conditions, the details have to be considered to determine whether an appeal is desirable. At the outset, it will be necessary to decide if it is appropriate to instruct counsel. As an interim measure advice can be obtained from various expert witnesses and counsel asked to advise as to merits. If an appeal is decided upon, the grounds of appeal will have to be settled. This will normally be done by counsel in consultation with the lay client and the expert witnesses and will involve a detailed traversal of the grounds for refusal. It is, however, possible to set out a general ground of appeal and reserve the right to supply further details in due course.

The notice of appeal (which is lodged in duplicate) is in form TCP 201 and can be obtained, together with other relevant forms, from the Department of the Environment. The form requires the applicant to state whether he requires the appeal to be heard by way of written representations. Such procedure is only suitable for appeals of a straightforward kind. For further details see circular 38/81, 'Planning and enforcement appeals'.

Supporting documents to be lodged with the notice of appeal are set out in art 20(2) of the GDO 1977 and also in the form TCP 201 and consist of:

(*a*) a copy of the application made to the local planning authority;

(*b*) a copy of—

(i) any s 27 certificate submitted to the local planning authority;

(ii) any notice and the relevant certificate provided in accordance with s 26 of the Act;

(iii) any industrial development certificate or office development permit submitted to the local planning authority (if applicable);

(*c*) a copy of all the relevant plans, drawings, particulars and other documents submitted with the application;

(*d*) a copy of the notice of the authority's decision, if any;

(*e*) copies of the outline planning application and permission (if the appeal concerns reserved matters);

(*f*) copies of all relevant correspondence with the local planning authority.

No fee is payable and there is no need to notify the local planning authority involved.

5 Conduct of the appeal

The procedure at an inquiry is governed by the Town and Country Planning (Inquiries Procedure) Rules 1974 (SI 1974 No 419) and, where appropriate, the Town and Country Planning Appeals (Determination by Appointed Persons) (Inquiries Procedure) Rules 1974 (SI 1974 No 420). The former rules are here referred to, and r 5(1) provides that a date, time and place shall be fixed for the holding of the inquiry and may be varied by the Secretary of State who shall give not less than forty-two days notice in writing of such date, time and place to the applicant and to the local planning authority, and to all s 29 parties (as defined by r 3(1)) at the addresses furnished by them. The procedure may be varied with the consent of the parties. In practice, there is usually a considerable delay, in the case of an important appeal, before the appellant receives notice of the hearing date, and from the notification of the hearing date until the hearing itself. Such time will give the expert witnesses an opportunity of investigating the appeal in detail and conferring with counsel as to advice on evidence. The witnesses necessary to an appeal involving residential development will depend on the importance and complexity of the appeal. The appellant, or possibly his architect, will have to give evidence as to the general background of the appellant's activities and of the appeal itself. In addition, it may be necessary for experts in planning, economics and traffic to be called. In the case of an appeal involving agricultural land, evidence will have to be given as to the type and quality of the agricultural land and its suitability for housing as opposed to agriculture. Under r 6(1) where an application has been referred to the Secretary of State he shall (where this has not already been done) not later than twenty-eight days before the date of the inquiry, serve or cause to be served on the appellant, the local authority, and the s 29 parties, a written statement of the reasons for his direction that the application be referred to him, and any points which seem to him to be likely to be relevant to his consideration of the application. Similarly, by r 6(2) the local planning authority shall not later than twenty-eight days before the date of the inquiry serve on the appellant and the s 29 parties a written statement of any submission which the local planning authority propose to put forward at the inquiry and supply a copy to the Secretary of State. 'The rule 6 statement' shall include a list of the documents intended to be put in evidence at the inquiry(r 6(4)). In certain cases the appellant may be required to prepare a r 6 statement if so required by the Secretary of State (r 6(6)). Failure to serve the r 6 statement within the time specified, or alterations or additions to it, may be a ground for adjournment of the appeal (r 10(5)).

The r 6 statement should be carefully perused by the appellants and their advisers in order that the final proofs of evidence can be prepared to deal with any difficult points which are revealed. To expedite the conduct of the appeal it may be possible for the parties to exchange various proofs of evidence prior to the commencement of the appeal. Such exchange should, however, be done on a mutual, not a unilateral, basis. The expert witnesses should be requested to prepare additional copies of their proofs for distribution at the hearing to the inspector, the opposition, the press and other interested parties.

It may be possible for certain matters to be dealt with between the parties before the inquiry. For example, problems can be identified by the expert witnesses and solutions agreed upon. Data can be agreed although it is advisable that this be confirmed in writing. A s 52 agreement (see Chapter 2, head 4 (*d*)) can be entered into conditional upon planning consent being granted, eg in relation to road improvements.

At the inquiry the appellant's counsel will open his case and then call his witnesses who will be cross examined by the local planning authority. The authority will then call their witnesses and their counsel will conduct his examination in chief followed by cross examination. Other interested parties will then be heard. The local planning authority's counsel will sum up and finally the appellant's counsel will sum up (r 10(2)). The persons entitled to appear at an inquiry are defined by r 7. By r 10(1) the procedure at the inquiry shall be such as the inspector shall in his discretion determine. Such discretion has been upheld by the courts as in *T A Miller* v *Minister of Housing and Local Government* [1968] 1 WLR 992 where Lord Denning observed: 'A tribunal of this kind is the master of its own procedure provided that the rules of natural justice are applied.' In practice the procedure is relatively informal eg hearsay evidence is admissible. For further details of procedure at an inquiry see r 10(3) to (8). Site inspection is dealt with by r 11. Rules 12 and 13 set out the procedure after the inquiry and the notification of the decision. In practice there will be considerable delay before the result of the appeal is notified to the parties.

Section 1(1) of the Planning Inquiries (Attendance of Public) Act 1982 provides that at any public inquiry oral evidence shall be heard in public and documentary evidence shall be open to public inspection. Certain exceptions to the general rule are set out in s 1(2), (3) and include, for example, the national interest. For further guidance in regard to the conduct of an appeal see ministerial circular 38/81, 'Planning and enforcement appeals'.

6 Costs

The Secretary of State has power to award costs (s 250(5) of the Local Government Act 1972; s 282 of the Town and Country Planning Act 1971). Such awards are at the discretion of the minister (*Re Wood's Application* (1952) 3 P & CR 238) and the principles involved are set out in circulars 73/65 and 69/71. Usually an award will only be made when the party has acted unreasonably as, for example, where he has made repeated applications on the same site.

7 Appeal to the High Court

By s 245(1) of the Town and Country Planning 1971 Act any person who: (*a*) is aggrieved by any order to which the section applies and desires to question the validity of that order, on the grounds that the order is not within the powers of the Act, or that any of the relevant requirements have not been complied with in relation to that order; or (*b*) is aggrieved by any action on the part of the Secretary of State to which this section applies and desires to question the validity of that action, on the grounds that the action is not within the powers of this Act, or that any of the relevant requirements have not been complied with in relation to that action, may, within six weeks from the date on which the order is confirmed or the action is taken, as the case may be, make an application to the High Court under this section. For the definition of 'the relevant requirements' see s 245(7). The six weeks' period for the lodging of the appeal runs from the date of the minister's decision letter, not the date of the receipt by the appellant (*Griffiths* v *Secretary of State for the Environment* [1983] 2 AC 51, HL). The two grounds therefore on which a decision of the Minister can be attacked are (*a*) ultra vires and (*b*) a breach of the procedural requirements. For example the refusal of an adjournment may be unreasonable (*Gill & Co (London)* v *Secretary of State for the Environment* [1978] JPL 373), as may the refusal to give an objector the opportunity of cross-examining a local authority witness (*Nicholson* v *Secretary of State for Energy* [1978] JPL 39) and failure of the Inspector to report adequately on the issues involving a residential development (*East Hampshire District Council* v *Secretary of State for the Environment* [1978] JPL 182). Failure to take into account a material ministerial circular will cause a decision to be quashed (*CJA Pye (Oxford) Estates Ltd* v *West Oxfordshire District Council* (1982) JPL 577). For a useful summary of the principles upon which the minister's decision can be challenged, see the judgment of Forbes J in *Seddon Properties Ltd and James Crosbie & Sons Ltd* v *Secretary of State for the Environment and Another* (1978) 248 EG 951. In conclusion, challenge on the merits is, however, likely to prove unfruitful.

Chapter 7

Building Regulations

1 General

In this chapter the Public Health Act 1936, the Public Health Act 1961 and the Health and Safety at Work Act 1974 are described as the 1936 Act, the 1961 Act and the 1974 Act respectively.

By s 61 of the 1974 Act (substituting s 61 of the 1936 Act) subject to the provisions of Pt II of the 1961 Act the Secretary of State has power to make regulations in respect of the design and construction of buildings (as defined by s 74(1) of the 1974 Act) and the provision of services, fittings and equipment in or in connection with buildings. As the sanctions for contravention of building regulations can be severe (see head 6 below) it is essential, not only for the builder who wishes to sell newly constructed houses, but also for a prospective purchaser of such a house, to ensure that the necessary formalities have been complied with.

The purposes for which regulations can be made are defined by s 61(2) as securing the health, safety, welfare and convenience of persons in or about buildings and of others who may be affected by buildings or matters connected with buildings; furthering the conservation of fuel and power; and preventing waste, undue consumption, misuse or contamination of water. By s 61(3) building regulations may provide for particular requirements of the regulations to be deemed to be complied with where prescribed methods of construction, prescribed types of materials or other prescribed means are used in or in connection with buildings; and regulations may be framed to any extent by reference to a document published by or on behalf of the Secretary of State or any other person or body, or by reference to the approval or satisfaction of any prescribed person or body. Under s 61(4) building regulations may include provision as to the giving of notices; the deposit and retention of plans; the inspection and testing of work, and the taking of samples. Schedule 5 to the 1974 Act sets out in detail the subject-matter of building regulations. Exemptions from building regulations are dealt with by s 61(5) and (6). Section 61 of the 1974 Act (also substituting s 62 of the 1936 Act) makes provision for building regulations to be applicable to (inter alia) alterations and extensions to existing buildings. Section 70(1) of the 1974 Act gives power to make building regulations for Inner London. The regulations presently applicable are the Building Regulations 1976 (SI 1976 No 1676) ('the 1976 Regulations') as amended by the Building (First Amendment) Regulations 1978 (SI 1978 No 723) relating to the conservation of fuel and power, the Building (Second Amendment) Regulations 1981 (SI 1981 No 1338) ('the 1981 Regulations') and the Building (Third Amendment) Regulations 1983 (SI 1983 No 195) which introduce further measures to control the insertion of insulating material into cavity walls. The 1976 Regulations as amended do not, however, apply to Inner London, where the appropriate byelaws will be applicable pursuant to the London Building Acts 1930 to 1978 and s 70(2), (3) of the 1974 Act. 'Inner London' means the area comprising the Inner London boroughs, the City, and the Inner Temple and the Middle Temple (s 70(7)).

2 Giving of notice and deposit of plans

By reg A10 of the 1976 Regulations as amended by reg 9 of the 1981 Regulations any person who intends to carry out an operation to which reg A6 (erection of buildings), A7 (alterations and extensions) or A8 (works and fittings) relates, or to make a material change of use to which reg A9 (material change of use) relates, shall give notice to the local authority and deposit plans in accordance with the relevant rules of Sched 3 if any substantive requirement of the Regulations applies to that operation or change of use, or the building is a building to which no such requirement applies and is a partially exempted building (as defined by the regulation) and is to be erected over a public sewer. By s 64(1) of the 1936 Act as substituted by s 25(1) of the Local Government (Miscellaneous Provisions) Act 1982, where plans of any proposed work are, in accordance with the building regulations, deposited with the local authority, the local authority is under a duty, subject to the provisions of the Act which expressly requires or authorises them in certain cases to reject plans, to pass the plans unless they either are defective, or show that the proposed work would contravene any of the building regulations. If the plans are defective or in contravention of any of the building regulations, the local authority may pursuant to s 64(1A) reject the plans or pass them subject to conditions. By s 64(1B) the conditions that can be imposed are such modifications to the deposited plans as the local authority may specify; and that such further plans as they may specify shall be deposited. A local authority may only pass plans subject to a condition specified in s 64(1B) if the person by or on whose behalf they were deposited has *in writing* requested them to do so or has consented to their doing so (s 64(1C), (1D)). Under s 64(2) of the 1936 Act as substituted by s 25(2), (2A) of the Local Government (Miscellaneous Provisions) Act 1982, the authority must within the prescribed period from the deposit of the plans give notice to the person by whom or on whose behalf they were deposited whether or not they have been passed, and a notice of rejection shall specify the defects on account of which the plans have been rejected, or the regulation or section of the Act for non-conformity with which, or under the authority of which, they have been rejected. The 'prescribed period' is five weeks or such extended period up to two months as the local authority may allow (s 64(4) of the 1936 Act and s 10(2) of the 1961 Act). A notice that plans have been passed shall specify any condition subject to which they have been passed, and shall state that the passing of the plans operates as an approval of them only for the purposes of the requirements of the regulations and the Act (s 25(2B)). Further by s 64(3) of the 1936 Act as substituted by Sched 6, Pt I, para 1, to the 1974 Act, where plans of any proposed work are rejected by the local authority there is a right of appeal against rejection to the Secretary of State within the prescribed time and in the prescribed manner. Where the rejection results wholly or partly from the fact that a person or body whose approval or satisfaction in any respect is required by the regulations has withheld approval or has not been satisfied, an appeal may be brought on (or on grounds which include) the ground that the person or body in question ought in the circumstances to have approved or been satisfied in that respect. See also s 69 of the 1974 Act for the procedural provisions relating to such an appeal. Powers to pass plans by stages or provisionally are given to the local authority by s 63(1), (3) of the 1974 Act. Furthermore, building regulations may impose continuing requirements to ensure that the provisions of the regulations are not frustrated (s 65 of the 1974 Act). Where deposited plans have been passed by the authority or notice of rejection has not been given within the prescribed period, and work has not been commenced within three years from the deposit of plans, the local authority may by notice declare the deposit of the plans shall be of no effect (s 66(1) of the 1936 Act and Sched 1, Pt III to the 1961 Act).

3 Fees

Section 62(3) of the 1974 Act authorises local authorities to charge prescribed fees in connection with the approval and passing of plans under the building regulations, and the present regulations are the Building (Prescribed Fees) Regulations 1982 (SI 1982 No 577). Regulation 8(*a*) provides the fees for the erection of small domestic buildings (as defined by reg 3) shall be fixed in accordance with Pt II of the Schedule to the Regulations by reference to the number of dwellings to be provided. In all other cases the fee is determined in accordance with Pt IV of the Schedule by reference to the estimated cost of the work.

4 Notice of commencement and completion

By reg A11(1), (2) of the 1976 Regulations (as amended by reg 10 of the 1981 Regulations), a builder carrying out or intending to carry out an operation coming within the scope of the regulations must furnish the local authority with not less than twenty-four hours' notice in writing of the date and time when the operation will commence. Not less than twenty-four hours' written notice must also be given before the covering up of any excavation for a foundation, any foundation, any damp-proof course or any concrete or other material laid over a site, or any work of haunching or covering in any way any drain or private sewer. Furthermore within seven days of the completion of such drainage works, notice to that effect must be given to the local authority. If the builder neglects or refuses to give any such notice, he shall comply with any notice in writing from the local authority requiring him within a reasonable time to cut into, lay open or pull down so much of the building, works or fittings as prevents the local authority from ascertaining whether any of the regulations have been contravened (reg A11(3)). Where the local authority has served a notice of contravention and the builder has complied with such notice, he shall within a reasonable time after the completion of the works give notice in writing to that effect to the local authority (reg A11(4)). The builder is also required to give notice in writing to the local authority of the erection, alteration or extension of a building and the execution of works or the installation of fittings in connection with a building, not more than seven days after completion (reg A11(5)). No form is prescribed for any notice to be given pursuant to reg A11 but such notice must be *in writing*.

5 Dispensation and relaxation

By s 6(1) of the 1961 Act (which, as amended by the 1974 Act, is set out in Sched 6, Pt II, to that Act) the Secretary of State, if he considers the operation of any requirement in building regulations would be unreasonable in relation to the particular case to which the application relates, may, after consultation with the local authority, give a direction dispensing with or relaxing that requirement either unconditionally or subject to compliance with any conditions specified in the direction, being conditions with respect to matters directly connected with the dispensation or relaxation. By s 6(2) of the 1961 Act and reg A13 of the 1976 Regulations as amended by reg 12 of the 1981 Regulations, the power under s 6(1) of the 1961 Act to dispense with or relax any requirement of the regulations shall be exercisable by the local authority (instead of the Secretary of State after consultation with the local authority) in relation to any application other than an application relating to reg E4 (provision of compartment walls and compartment floors) in respect of a building, or compartment, which exceeds or will exceed 7,000 m^3 in capacity. Regulation A12 of the 1976 Regulations as amended by reg 11 of the 1981 Regulations provides that any application for dispensing with or relaxation of the regulations shall be in duplicate in the appropriate forms as set out in Sched 4 to the regulations. The application by an individual is made to the local authority and, except when the power to dispense with or relax the regulations is vested in the local authority, such authority shall at once transmit the application to the Secretary of State and give notice to that effect to the applicant. Except where the local authority has the appropriate power, an application by such authority is made to the Secretary of State (s 6(5), (6) of the 1961 Act as amended). Section 8(1) of the 1961 Act requires the Minister or the local authority to advertise a proposal to relax the building regulations.

By s 7(1) of the 1961 Act (set out as amended in Pt II, Sched 6, to the 1974 Act) if a local authority refuse an application to dispense with or relax the building regulations, or grant such an application subject to conditions when empowered so to do, the applicant has a right of appeal to the Secretary of State within the period prescribed by the regulations and in the prescribed manner. Similarly there is a right of appeal if the local authority fail to give a decision on the application within the prescribed period (s 7(2)). See also s 69 of the 1974 Act for the procedural provisions relating to an appeal. If on application to the Secretary of State under s 6 he considers any requirement of the building regulations is not applicable, or is not or would not be contravened by the work or the proposed work, he may give a direction to that effect according to the circumstances (s 6(7A)). Furthermore s 66(1), (2) of the 1974 Act provides that if the Secretary of State considers the operation of any requirement of building regulations would be unreasonable in relation to any particular type of building matter, he may, either on application made to him or of his own accord, give a direction dispensing with or relaxing that requirement generally in relation to that type of building matter, either conditionally or unconditionally. Such a direction may provide that it ceases to have effect at the end of a specified period or it may be revoked by a subsequent direction.

6 Contravention

Section 65(1) of the 1936 Act (set out as amended in Pt II, Sched 6 to the 1974 Act) enacts that, if any work contravenes any of the building regulations, the authority, without prejudice to their right to take proceedings for a fine, may by notice require the owner either to pull down or remove the work or, if he so elects, to effect such alterations and additions as may be necessary to make it comply with the building regulations. Similar powers are vested in the authority if any work is executed either without plans having been deposited, or notwithstanding the rejection of the plans, or otherwise than in accordance with any requirements subject to which the authority passed the plans (s 65(2)). By s 65(2A) where a local authority have power to serve a notice under s 65(1) or (2) on the owner of any work, they may in addition or instead serve such a notice on the occupier and any builder or other person appearing to the authority to have control over the work or any one or more of them. Section 65(3) (as amended) provides that if a person fails to comply with the appropriate notice before the expiration of twenty-eight days, or such longer period as a court of summary jurisdiction may on his application allow, the local authority may pull down or remove the work in question, or effect such alterations therein and additions thereto and execute such additional work in connection therewith as they deem necessary, and may recover from him the expenses reasonably incurred by them in so doing. Where a notice is given to two or more persons in pursuance of s 65(2A), if they are given the notices on different dates, the period of twenty-eight days shall for each of them run from the later or latest of those dates. By s 65(4) (as amended by s 25(2) of the Local Government (Miscellaneous Provisions) Act 1982) no notice shall be given after the expiration of twelve months from the date of the completion of the work in question, and, in any case where plans were deposited and the work was shown on them, it shall not be open to the authority to give such a notice on the ground that the work contravenes any building regulation or, as the case may be, does not comply with their requirements under the Act, if either the plans were passed by the authority, or notice of their rejection was not given within the prescribed period from the deposit thereof, and if the work has been executed in accordance with the plans and of any requirement made by the local authority as a condition of passing the plans. However, in a case where plans were deposited and the work was shown on them, nothing in s 65(4) shall be taken to prevent such a notice from being given (before the expiration of twelve months from the completion of the work in question) in respect of anything of which particulars were not required to be shown in the plans. Furthermore, s 65(5) gives additional powers to the local authority or the Attorney-General or any other person to apply for an injunction for the removal or alteration of any work which contravenes the regulations. The court has power to order the local authority to pay compensation in the case of a wrongful application for an injunction.

For the fines payable if a person contravenes or fails to comply with the relevant building regulations, see s 4(6) of the 1961 Act as amended by Sched 6 to the 1974 Act and ss 38 and 46 of the Criminal Justice Act 1982.

Chapter 8

Road Charges

1 General

The purchaser of a newly constructed dwellinghouse, or a building plot, will require confirmation that the road abutting the property is adopted and maintained at the public expense, or alternatively that other adequate steps have been taken to ensure that there is no liability on him to meet the expenses of the construction of such road. Furthermore, he will need to know that the roads on the estate leading to his property from the nearest highway maintainable at the public expense are adopted, or will be adopted, in due course, when the estate has been completed or earlier if possible. The purchaser's mortgagee will also demand confirmation that these requirements have been satisfied. Building societies often make it a condition of their advance that there is an agreement pursuant to s 38 of the Highways Act 1980 whereby the builder constructs the estate roads; or that a deposit of monies has been made with the authority; or they will make an appropriate retention in respect of outstanding road works. A builder will, therefore, have to make appropriate provisions for the estate roads.

Where acquiring property by way of lease it should be noted that the normal clause as to payment of outgoings by the tenant may well render the tenant liable to meet road charge expenses: see *Wix v Rutson* [1899] 1 QB 474.

2 The advance payments code

(a) The general rule

The provisions of the advance payments code are set out in ss 219 to 225 of the Highways Act 1980 and are designed to have the effect of securing payment of the expenses of the execution of streetworks in private streets adjacent to new buildings. Section 219(1) provides for a sum to be secured or paid to the relevant street works authority in respect of any building which is planned to be built and will have a frontage on a private street in which the authority has power to execute works or require works to be executed. Subject to the exemptions contained in the section (see (*e*) below) no building work can be commenced until such security has been given or deposit paid. Contravention of the section is an offence (subs (2)). As to interest on sums paid under the advance payments code see s 225. For registration in the local land charges register see s 224. Section 1(2) of the Highways Act 1980 enacts that (except where the minister is responsible) the local highway authority for highways outside London shall be the county council.

(b) Determination of liability

Section 220(1), (2) provides that where the advance payments code is in force, the district council, in any case to which s 219 may be applicable, shall within one week of passing any plans for the erection of a building inform the street works authority. The street works authority shall then, within six weeks of the passing of the plans, serve a notice on the builder requiring payment or security for payment. The amount of the payment is determined by the streets works authority estimating the cost to them of making up the road to the standard of a public highway; it is this notional figure which is charged to the builder (see s 220(3)). As to the form and service of such notice see ss 320–2 of the Highways Act 1980.

The Act does not specify the type of security which may be given, but presumably a charge on building land would be adequate. For a precedent of a legal charge giving security under ss 219 and 220 see *The Encyclopaedia of Forms and Precedents*, 4th Ed, vol 10, p 197.

By s 220(4) the street works authority may subsequently reduce the sum or declare that no sum is payable by serving a notice, but the subsection does not apply when the authority have power to make a refund or release under s 221(1).

Section 220(7) provides for repayment of excess sums paid to the authority, and for the release of any security given. The section also deals with cases where land is subsequently divided into two or more parts thus creating two or more owners and the need for apportionment.

Section 220(6) gives a right of appeal to the minister against a notice, which right must be exercised not later than one month from the date of the service of the notice.

The purchaser should consider whether the sum deposited or secured is sufficient since he will be liable to make up any shortfall and if necessary should obtain an indemnity or make a retention on completion. Conversely, under certain circumstances, refunds are made and the contract should provide who is entitled to them. See also s 222(2) and *Henshall* v *Fogg* [1964] 1 WLR 1127.

(c) Refunds

By s 221 where a sum has been paid or secured under s 219 and the work has been done otherwise than at the expense of the street works authority a refund or release is made by the authority. The authority may refund or release in total or partially, according to the circumstances, and may also apportion a refund where land has been subsequently split. Where the person at whose expense the works were carried out is not the owner of the land, notification must be given to the owner before any refund or release is made.

A s 38 agreement may provide for a refund of the whole or part of the sum paid either without interest or with interest at such rate as may be specified in the agreement, or for the release of the whole or part of the security, as the case may be. As to the interest payable on refunds see s 225.

(d) Discharge and abortive development

Section 222(1), (2) provides that where a sum has been paid or secured for street works the developer's or subsequent owner's liability is discharged to the extent of the sum paid or secured, and if, when the street is declared to be a public highway, the sum is found to exceed the total liability in respect of the frontage, or there is no liability because the street was not made up at the expense of the street works authority, the street works authority shall either make the appropriate refund or release the security in whole or in part. Such refund is made to the person who is for the time being the owner of the land (s 222(2)). The section also deals with cases where land is subsequently divided into two or more parts thus creating two or more owners and the need for apportionment (s 222(3)).

Section 223(1), (2) deals with the situation where the developer gives notice to the local authority that he does not wish to proceed with the building or when the authority has declared under s 66 of the Public Health Act 1936 that the deposit of plans shall be of no effect. Where no building has begun, provision is made for the refund of any advance payment made or the release of any security given. The section also deals with cases where land is subsequently divided into two or more parts thus creating two or more owners and the need for apportionment.

(e) Exemptions from the code

Section 219(4) stipulates that the section shall not apply:

(i) in a case where the owner of the land on which the building is to be erected will be exempt from liability for street works, by virtue of a provision in the appropriate private street works code (eg the exemption for a place of public religious worship under s 215 of the Act);

(ii) in a case where the building proposed to be erected will be situated in the curtilage of, and be appurtenant to, an existing building;

(iii) in a case where the building is proposed to be erected in a parish or community and plans for the building were deposited with the district council or, according to the date of the deposit, the rural district council before the date on which the New Streets Act 1951, or the advance payments code (either in the Highways Acts 1959 or 1980) was applied in the parish or community, or as the case may require, in the part of the parish or community in which the building is to be erected;

(iv) in a case where an agreement has been made under s 38 of the Highways Act 1980 (see head 3 below);

(v) in a case where the street works authority is satisfied that the street, or the relevant part of it, is not, and is not likely within a reasonable time to be, substantially built up or in so unsatisfactory a condition as to justify the use of powers under the appropriate private street works code for securing the carrying out of street works in the street or part thereof, by notice exempt the building from this section;

(vi) in a case where the street works authority, being satisfied that the street is not, and is not likely within a reasonable time to become, joined to a highway maintainable at the public expense, by notice exempt the building from this section;

(vii) in a case where the whole street, being less than one hundred yards in length, or a part of the street not less than one hundred yards in length, and comprising the whole of the part on which the frontage of the building will be, was, on the material date (as defined by s 219(6)), built up to such extent that the aggregate length of the frontages of the building on both sides of the street or part constituted at least one half of the aggregate length of all the frontages on both sides of the street or part;

(viii) in a case (not falling within exception (vii)) where the street works authority, being satisfied that the whole of the street was on the material date, substantially built up, by notice exempt the building;

(ix) in a case where the building is proposed to be erected on land belonging to or in the possession of the British Transport Boards, a county or district or London borough, the Greater London Council, the Common Council of the City of London, or a new town development corporation;

(x) in a case where the building is proposed to be erected by a company the objects of which include the provision of industrial premises (as defined by s 203(3)) for use by persons other than the company, and the constitution of which prohibits the distribution of the profits of the company to its members, and the cost of building is to be defrayed wholly or mainly by a government department;

(xi) in a case where the street works authority, is satisfied: (a) that more than three quarters of the aggregate length of all the frontages on both sides of the street, or a part of the street not less than one hundred yards in length and comprising the whole of the part on which the frontage of the building will be, consists, or is at some future time likely to consist, of the frontages of industrial premises; and (b) that their powers under the appropriate private street works code are not likely to be exercised in relation to the street, or to that part, within a reasonable time, by resolution exempt the street or part of the street.

It should be noted that there is an automatic exemption in cases (i), (ii), (iii), (iv), (vii), (ix), (x) and only a discretionary exemption in the case of (v), (vi), (viii), (xi).

3 Section 38 Agreements

The commonest exemption to a deposit or a provision of security under s 219(4) is an agreement entered into under s 38 of the Highways Act 1980. Such an agreement may avoid the builder having to make capital available for deposit or provide other security. Furthermore, it will probably be less expensive for the builder to carry out the work himself rather than the highway authority.

By s 38(1) where a person is liable to maintain a highway, the minister, in the case of a trunk road, or the local highway authority, in any other case, may agree with that person to undertake the maintenance of the highway. Where an agreement is made the highway shall, on a specified date, become a highway maintainable at the public expense. By s 38(3) a local highway authority may agree with any person, as from a certain date, to undertake the maintenance of a private carriage or occupation road which that person, provided he has the power to do so, is willing to dedicate as a highway. The subsection also applies to any way which *is to be* constructed by a person, or by a highway authority on his behalf, and which the person *proposes* to dedicate as a highway. Section 38(6) provides that the agreement may contain such provisions as the authority think fit; in practice, fairly stringent provisions will be incorporated. For precedents of such agreements see *The Encyclopaedia of Forms and Precedents*, 4th Ed, vol 10, pp 98–111.

The purchaser will have to approve the terms of the agreement and to confirm that it covers all roads on the estate which lead to a public highway. The Law Society have recommended (see *Law Society's Gazette*, vol 62, p 537) that the vendor's solicitor should supply, free of charge, the following:

(a) a copy of the agreement and bond or an abstract, and a copy of the site plan or an appropriate extract;

(b) the vendor's part agreement for inspection and give an acknowledgment for production;

(c) an appropriate authorisation to the highway authority to allow inspection of the originals or to give particulars required by the purchaser or his mortgagee. The recommendation does not however extend to the production of plans and specifications.

See also Practice Notes in *Law Society's Gazette*, vol 75, p 1168 and vol 77, p 142.

The purchaser should check that the agreement is supported by a bond given by an insurance company or bank as security for the road works being satisfactorily carried out. In practice, it is most unusual for a bond to be dispensed with. If a builder is financially sound it is not difficult to obtain a bond and advice should be obtained from an insurance broker as to the companies which specialise in underwriting this type of business. In the case of a subsidiary company of a larger group the insurance company may require a counter indemnity from the parent company before granting a bond to the subsidiary. For consideration of the respective obligations of a builder surety and local authority under a s 38 agreement see *National Employers' Mutual General Insurance Association v Herne Bay UDC* (1972) 70 LGR 542.

By way of further protection the purchaser may also request the vendor to give a covenant and indemnity in the conveyance to make up the roads to a standard required by the local authority within a specified period, and to be responsible for any road charges. Such covenant may not be of much practical use, however, if the builder is a man of straw. See also *Halsall v Brizell* [1957] Ch 169 as to the enforceability of such a covenant against the covenantor's successor in title.

Chapter 9

Defective Building

1 Survey

Prior to signing the contract for the purchase of a newly constructed house it is always advisable for the purchaser to have the property surveyed by a surveyor instructed on his behalf. Moreover, when a building society is involved they will insist on a survey. In *Yianni* v *Edwin Evans & Sons* [1981] 3 WLR 843 it was held that a building society surveyor owes a duty of care to a purchaser/borrower in addition to the building society. Such purchaser/borrower can therefore rely on the contents of the building society survey, and in the event of suffering loss due to professional negligence can accordingly sue the surveyor in question for damages. As to the measure of such damages see *Perry* v *Sidney Phillips & Son (a firm)* (1982) 263 EG 888, CA. When a building society is not involved and an independent survey has been carried out the surveyor's report should be critically studied, particularly in view of the fact that there is a growing tendency for some surveyors to include in their report wide qualifications excluding liability wholly or in part. As to a solicitor's duty to his client in respect of surveys, see *Buckland* v *Mackesy* (1968) 208 EG 969.

2 Contract

(a) Express provision

Where a building agreement has been entered into for the construction of a dwellinghouse, express provision can be inserted in the agreement to ensure that the house will be constructed in a satisfactory manner, for example, in accordance with plans and specifications attached to the agreement, and to the satisfaction of the purchaser's surveyor. However, such plans and specifications must be comprehensive and not themselves defective in any way. In *Lynch* v *Thorne* [1956] 1 WLR 303 where a builder agreed to construct a house with a nine inch brick wall, in accordance with the terms of the contract, and this did not provide adequate weather proofing, it was held that the purchaser could not complain that the builder was in breach of his obligations. Against this can be contrasted the Canadian case of *Brunswick Construction Letee* v *Nowlan* (1974) 49 DLR (3d) 93 where it was held that a builder who strictly follows an architect's plans and specifications may still be liable if they were manifestly incorrect. Compare also s 1(2) and (3) of the Defective Premises Act 1972, see head 3(*b*) below. Subject to contrary provision, clauses as to the construction and making good of any defects contained in the contract will not merge on the completion of the conveyance, lease, or transfer (*Hancock* v *B W Brazier (Anerley) Ltd* [1966] 1 WLR 1317). In *Billyack* v *Leyland Construction Co Ltd* [1968] 1 WLR 471 there was a clause that the property should be built in 'a good and workmanlike manner' and that the local authority's habitation certificate was to be conclusive evidence of completion of the house; this was held to establish the completion date of the conveyance and did not preclude a further action for bad workmanship. As to the liability of a builder and developer in contract *and* tort, and as to defects in surrounding land see *Batty* v *Metropolitan Property Realisations Ltd* [1978] QB 554.

(b) Implied warranties in building agreements

In the case of a building agreement or the purchase of a dwelling-house in the course of erection there is an implied warranty at common law that (*a*) the house will be constructed in a proper and workmanlike manner; (*b*) the builder will supply good and proper materials; and (*c*) the house will be reasonably fit for human habitation (*Miller* v *Cannon Hill Estates Ltd* [1931] 2 KB 113). There will be *no* implied warranty if the house is *completed* before the signature of the contract for purchase, even though the property is on a building estate (*Hoskins* v *Woodham* [1938] 1 All ER 692). The implied warranty can be excluded by express stipulation (*Hancock* v *B W Brazier (Anerley) Ltd* above). The implied warranty is not broken if the builder complies with plans and specifications as in *Lynch* v *Thorne*.

3 Tort and breach of statutory duty

(a) Negligence

At common law a builder can be liable in negligence for a defective building (*Dutton* v *Bognor Regis UDC* [1972] 1 QB 373). See also *Anns* v *Merton London Borough Council* [1978] AC 728, HL. Furthermore a subcontractor of the main building contractor owes a duty of care to a third party for whom a building is being constructed, and will be liable for economic and financial loss arising as a result of such breach of duty even though there is no contractual relationship between the subcontractor and the third party (*Junior Books Ltd v Veitchi Co Ltd* [1982] 3 WLR 477, HL).

(b) Defective Premises Act 1972

The common law position has been reinforced by the Defective Premises Act 1972 which came into force on 1 January 1974. Section 1(1) provides that a person taking on work for, or in connection with, the provision of a dwelling (whether by the erection or the conversion or enlargement of a building) owes a duty if the dwelling is provided to the order of any person, to that person and to every person who acquires an interest (whether legal or equitable) in the dwelling, to see that the work which he takes on is done in a workmanlike or professional manner, with proper materials so that it will be fit for habitation when completed. It should be noted that the section is not limited to houses in the course of construction as in the case of the implied contractual warranty. Further, the section is seemingly not limited to builders, but extends to architects, surveyors and other professional advisers.

By s 1(2) a person who takes on any such work for another on terms that he is to do it in accordance with instructions given by, or on behalf of, that other shall, to the extent to which he does it properly, in accordance with those instructions, be treated as discharging the duty which has been imposed on him by s 1(1), except where he owes a duty to that other to warn him of any defects in the instructions, and fails to discharge that duty. A person shall not be treated as having given instructions for doing the work merely because he has agreed to the work being done in the specified manner, with specified materials, or to a specified design (s 1(3)). The duty imposed by the section applies to a person whose business consists of, or includes, providing or arranging for the provision of dwellings, or installations in dwellings, or in the exercise of a statutory power of making such provision or arrangements arranges for another to take on the work for, or in connection with, the provision of a dwelling (s 1(4)); thus the duty would extend to a local authority providing council houses.

Section 2 provides certain cases to be excluded from the duty under s 1. In particular, s 2(1)–(6) excludes approved schemes ie the ten year protection scheme of the National House-Building Council, whereby the builder gives warranties in similar terms to those contained in s 1 (see head 4(d) below). See also House-Building

Standards (Approved Scheme etc) Order 1979 (SI 1979 No 381).
Section 1 is also excluded in certain cases where land is compulsorily
acquired (s 2(7)).

Under s 3(1) any duty of care owed in connection with building
work to persons who might reasonably be expected to be affected
by defects in the state of the premises created by doing the work
shall not be abated by the subsequent disposal (as defined by s 6(1))
of the premises by the person who owed the duty. The section is
subject to certain exceptions contained in subs (2).

Section 6(2) enacts that any duty imposed by the Act is in
addition to any duty a person may owe apart from the Act. Any
term of an agreement which purports to exclude or restrict, or has
the effect of excluding or restricting, the operation of the Act, or
any liability arising by virtue of such provision shall be void (s 6(3)).

(c) Local authorities

A local authority may be liable in negligence or breach of statutory duty. In *Anns* v *Merton London Borough Council* [1978] AC 728,
HL, the facts were that in 1962 the appellant local council approved
building plans for a block of flats, the construction of which was
completed that year. In 1970 cracking and other damage became
apparent. In 1972 the lessees sued the council (inter alia) alleging
negligence and failure to inspect the building properly, or at all, so
as to ensure that the foundations were in accordance with the
approved plans. The House of Lords considered whether the council
was under a duty of care. It was held that: (i) under the Public
Health Act 1936 the council had a power, as opposed to a duty, to
inspect building work to ensure compliance with the byelaws; (ii)
failure to carry out inspection would not render the council liable
unless it proved that they had failed to exercise properly their
discretion not to make inspection, and they failed to exercise reasonable care to ensure compliance with the byelaws; (iii) where such
inspections were carried out the council retained a discretion as to
the manner in which inspections were performed; if such discretion
were not bona fide exercised the council might be liable in negligence for failing to take reasonable care. See also *Dutton* v *Bognor
Regis UDC* [1972] 1 QB 373; *Sparham-Souter* v *Town and Country
Developments (Essex) Ltd* [1976] QB 858; and *Acrecrest Ltd* v *W S
Hattrell & Partners and Another* [1982] 3 WLR 1076, CA, where
liability was apportioned between the local authority and the architects involved; also *Worlock* v *Saws (a firm) and Another* (1983) 265
EG 776, CA, as to apportionment of liability between the local
authority and the builder.

(d) Limitation of actions

Under ss 2 and 5 of the Limitation Act 1980 the normal period of limitation in actions founded on tort or simple contract is six years from the date on which the cause of action accrued. In *Pirelli General Cable Works Ltd v Oscar Faber & Partners* [1983] 2 WLR 6, HL, the defendant firm of consulting engineers designed a chimney for the plaintiffs. The design was negligent, and the chimney was built during June and July 1969. Damage in the form of cracks near the top of the chimney occurred not later than April 1970, and the writ was issued more than eight years later in October 1978. The damage was not discovered until November 1977 and the defendants had not established that the plaintiffs ought reasonably to have discovered the damage before October 1972—six years before the issue of the writ. The House of Lords held the cause of action accrued when the damage came into existence in April 1970 and accordingly was statute barred. Their lordships, however, observed that such a result was unreasonable and reform by Parliament might soon be expected.

However by s 8 of the Limitation Act 1980 an action upon a specialty (ie a contract under seal) shall not be brought after the expiration of twelve years from the date on which the cause of action accrued. In view of the uncertain state of the law, a prudent purchaser may require a building contract with the developer to be under seal so as to give the additional protection of a longer period of limitation.

Reference should also be made to s 1(5) of the Defective Premises Act 1972 which provides that any cause of action in respect of a breach of duty imposed by the section shall be deemed to have accrued at the time when the dwelling was completed, but if after that time a person who has done work for, or in connection with the provision of the dwellinghouse, does further work to rectify the work he has already done, any such cause of action in respect of that further work shall be deemed for those purposes to have accrued at the time when the further work was finished.

4 National House-Building Council scheme

(a) General

The general object of the National House-Building Council is to ensure the purchaser of a new house, which is constructed by a builder or developer registered under the scheme, is not prejudiced if the house is built in a defective manner. If a new dwelling is so built the Council operates an insurance scheme to protect the purchaser under the National House-Building Council Rules (form HBI, 1979 Ed), the current set of which came into force on 18 April 1979. A copy of the Rules can be obtained from the Registrar's Department, National House-Building Council, Chiltern Avenue, Amersham, Bucks HP6 5AP.

The Council also adopts various methods of ensuring that its requirements as to building are observed by means of inspection and disciplinary action. The ultimate sanction is for a builder or developer to be struck off the register. Such an action will seriously prejudice his trading prospects, since building societies now usually insist on new dwellings being protected under the scheme before agreeing to the advance of mortgage monies. Furthermore, provision has been made to protect purchasers against the effects of inflation whereby the Council's liability is linked to the United Kingdom Housing Cost Index prepared by the Building Cost Information Service of the Royal Institution of Chartered Surveyors (see ss II and III of the House Purchaser's Insurance Policy form HB7). Where appropriate the insurance cover extends to the common parts (as defined by Rule 47) of a flat or maisonette. What follows is a brief summary of the effects of the scheme.

(b) Application for membership

Rule 47 defines a house-builder as any person, partnership, company or organization engaged in the construction of dwellings. A developer is defined as any person, partnership, company or organization that arranges for the construction of dwellings or is concerned in or with such arrangements. Any person falling within the definition may apply to the Council to have his name entered on the register (Rule 1(a)). Every application for registration shall be made on the form prescribed by the Council and shall be accompanied by a non-returnable application fee of £100 or such other fee as the Council may determine. The Council may reject the application, grant it unconditionally or grant it subject to conditions (Rule 5). Rule 6 then sets out in detail the conditions which the Council may require to impose before an applicant's name is entered on the register, for example, service of a probationary period, cash deposits, guarantees and indemnities. As to the subsequent liability of the directors of a newly formed housebuilding company in regard to a guarantee given to the National House-Building Council on the initial application to register the company, see *National House-Building Council* v *Fraser and Another* (1983) 133 NLJ 376. For rights of appeal against the Council's decision, see Rule 36. In particular Rule 36(c) requires notice of appeal to be given to the Council within *fourteen* days of receiving notice of the decision appealed against and shall not be valid unless accompanied by £250 (or such other sum as the Council may determine) as security for the Council's cost of the appeal.

(c) Obligations of developer or house-builder to offer an agreement and deliver an insurance policy to the purchaser

Rule 18(*a*)–(*c*) deals with the obligation of the developer or house-builder to make an irrevocable offer to enter into an agreement with the purchaser in the current form HB5 (1979 Ed). Rule 18(*c*) extends the obligation to house purchaser's agreements for public authorities (forms HB5B and C). Rule 19 deals with partly constructed dwellings. A specific clause should be inserted in the contract of sale of a dwelling so as to comply with Rule 18. Rule 21 provides that on the signing of the agreement the insurance policy shall forthwith be delivered to the purchaser. On a house-builder or developer complying with his obligations under the Rules the Council issues a standard notice of insurance cover (form HB6) and in appropriate cases a common parts notice of insurance cover (Rule 22(*a*)(i)). This notice brings into operation the insurance benefits as set out in the insurance policy. A declaration of purchase price (form HB6P (1980)) is attached to the standard notice of insurance cover and must be completed and returned to the NHBC so that the insurance cover of the dwelling can be recorded.

(d) Vendor's warranties

The vendor's warranties are set out in clauses 2, 3, 4, 6 and 9 of the House Purchaser's Agreement form HB5 (1979 Ed). The two important obligations in relation to defective building are set out in clauses 3 and 6 of the agreement. First, the vendor warrants that the dwelling has been built, or will be built, in an efficient and workmanlike manner and of proper materials and so as to be fit for habitation. Secondly, the vendor warrants that he shall within a reasonable time and at his own expense remedy any defects in the dwelling caused by a breach of the Council's requirements and any damage to the dwelling caused by such defect provided that such defect or damage first appears and is reported to the vendor *in writing* within the initial guarantee period, ie two years from the date of issue of the notice of insurance cover or, where the dwelling has been unoccupied for twelve months or more from such date, one year from the first purchase of the dwelling. Furthermore if works undertaken by the vendor within the initial guarantee period fail to remedy such defects or damage, the vendor remains under a continuing liability to remedy them even after the expiration of the initial guarantee period. The warranties are subject to certain

qualifications and also limitations as to liability. For full details of
the vendor's warranties and the procedure involved in the written
notification of a breach of the warranties, the reader is referred to
form HB5.

(e) *Liabilities of the Council under the insurance policy*

Briefly where loss occurs before issue of notice of insurance cover
the Council will pursuant to s I of the policy (form HB7(2)) give
certain protection against loss caused by the vendor's failure due to
his bankruptcy, liquidation or fraud to commence or to complete
the construction of the dwelling. Special conditions are attached to
the section which exclude the Council's liability. Section II deals
with the loss during the initial guarantee period and provides that
the Council will pay the purchaser the costs of remedying any defect
or damage which first appears and is reported to the vendor *in
writing* within the initial guarantee period and which the vendor
fails to remedy in accordance with clause 6 of the House Purchaser's
Agreement. Again special conditions are attached to the section
which exclude the Council's liability. Section III deals with loss
occurring during the structural guarantee period, ie the period
commencing upon the expiry of the initial guarantee period and
expiring ten years from the date of issue of the notice of insurance
cover. Under the section the Council will pay the purchaser the cost
of remedying (*a*) major damage which appears and is reported
during the structural guarantee period and is caused by any defect
in the structure or by subsidence, settlement or heave; and (*b*) any
such defect, subsidence, settlement or heave but only where such
major damage has appeared provided that such cost is not covered
by other insurance at the time of the claim. The section contains
further detailed provisions dealing with the special and general
exclusions of liability and limitations on liability.

(f) *Third parties*

The problem arises as to whether a purchaser from the original
purchaser of a new dwelling house will be covered by an NHBC
agreement and insurance policy and accordingly receive the appropriate protection under the scheme. Rule 41 provides that a
house-builder or developer shall not seek to deny liability under the
Rules or under any house purchaser's agreement on the grounds
that such agreement has not been assigned. Furthermore clause 10
of form HB5 provides that the agreement is made by the first
purchaser on behalf of himself and his successors in title and his
and their mortgagees in possession. The vendor also undertakes

that he will not seek to deny liability under the agreement on the ground that it has not been assigned.

Although as a result of Rule 41 and clause 10 it would seem unnecessary for a second purchaser to receive a formal assignment, it is submitted nevertheless that a solicitor acting in such circumstances may deem it prudent to insist on a formal assignment and also serve an appropriate notice of assignment thus avoiding doubt and uncertainty. Provision as to assignment can be made by incorporating an appropriate clause in the contract of sale of the dwelling. Furthermore, the insurance policy should be produced for inspection, enquiries should be made as to whether any defects have been reported in writing in accordance with the terms of the agreement and full details of all copy correspondence and documentation relating thereto should be obtained.

Chapter 10

Miscellanea

1 Pooling agreements

In times of economic hardship when it is difficult for purchasers to obtain mortgages, a builder may wish to assist the sale of houses by entering into a 'pooling agreement' with a building society. Under such an agreement the society advances loans to the purchasers of newly erected houses on the security of a high proportion of the value of the house, and the builder deposits with the society by way of collateral charge, funds to ensure that the purchasers meet their commitments under the mortgage. Such agreements come within the meaning of 'continuing arrangements', which is defined by s 129(1) of the Building Societies Act 1962 as 'any arrangement made between a building society and another person whereby, in contemplation of a series of advances comprising excess advances being made by the society to members for the purpose of their being used in defraying the purchase price of freehold or leasehold estates, that person undertakes to give the society a series of guarantees, each of which is to secure sums payable to the society in respect of such an advance'. The section also defines 'excess advance' as 'the amount by which the advance exceeds the basic advance' and 'basic advance' as meaning, in relation to any advance made or to be made for the purpose of its being used to defray the purchase price of freehold or leasehold estate, 'the maximum amount which the building society would consider proper to advance on the security of that estate, if no other security were taken by the society'. The Fourth Schedule of the 1962 Act provides for the guarantees to be given under continuing arrangements. Part I deals with the general requirements. Part II outlines exemptions from certain requirements in the case of continuing arrangements with government departments and other bodies. Part III deals with the modification of requirements in certain other cases. The requirements set out in the Fourth Schedule are complicated and the reader is referred to its provisions for full details. For a precedent of a pooling agreement see *The Encyclopaedia of Forms and Precedents*, 4th Ed, vol 3, p 763.

2 Conflict of interest

The practice has lately arisen whereby a vendor building company will agree to pay a purchaser's solicitor's costs in regard to the acquisition of a newly constructed house. This can give rise to a possible conflict of interest for the solicitor concerned and the Council of the Law Society made a statement regarding the matter in the *Law Society's Gazette*, vol 79, p 187, from which the following is a relevant extract:

There is no basic objection to a solicitor acting for a purchaser where the vendor has agreed to pay the purchaser's legal costs. However, the Council are concerned to ensure that where the vendor building company is recommending a number of purchaser clients to a given firm, no conflict of interest should arise between the solicitor's duty to the purchaser client and his desire to remain on the building company's panel of recommended solicitors.

A purchaser's solicitor who knowingly, and as a matter of prior or existing arrangement with the vendor, has purchasers effectively introduced by the vendor as prospective clients, is, in the opinion of the Council, at grave risk of being unable to provide the level of independent and objective service to which they are entitled and which the solicitor should render as a matter of professional duty.

In this connection the attention of solicitors who are so approached by a building company is drawn to r 1 of the Solicitors Practice Rules 1936/72. The essential principle of r 1 in this particular context is that purchasers should not be unduly influenced in their choice of solicitor.

Any solicitor who accepts instructions from purchasers under the circumstances outlined above, or indeed in any similar circumstances (and whether or not they have agreed to do the work at a special fee) will be at serious risk of being in breach of the rule, because such circumstances might well amount to an arrangement for the recommendation to the solicitor of prospective purchasers. This type of arrangement is one of the examples of the breach of r 1 quoted on p 185 of *A Guide to the Professional Conduct of Solicitors*.

3 Builder's rubbish

Builders are inclined to leave newly erected properties and, particularly, unmade gardens in an untidy state. It is suggested that to avoid such difficulty the purchaser may seek to have the following clause inserted in the contract: 'Forthwith upon the completion of the dwellinghouse and prior to the completion of the conveyance to the purchaser the vendor hereby undertakes (*a*) to remove all rubbish and other materials from the said dwellinghouse and to leave the same in a clean and tidy condition to the satisfaction of the purchaser, and (*b*) to remove all rubble and other surplus materials from the garden of the said dwellinghouse and generally to leave the garden in a clean and tidy condition to the satisfaction of the purchaser.'

4 Builder's skips

Section 139(11) of the Highways Act 1980 defines a 'builder's skip' as 'a container designed to be carried on a road vehicle and to be placed on a highway or other land for the storage of builders' materials, or for the removal and disposal of builders' rubble, waste, household and other rubbish or earth'. Section 139(1) of the Act provides that a builder's skip shall not be deposited on a highway without the permission of the relevant highway authority. Such permission can be granted subject to conditions (see s 139(2)). By s 139(4) where permission has been granted the owner of the skip shall secure that (*a*) the skip is properly lighted during the hours of darkness; (*b*) the skip is clearly and indelibly marked with the owner's name and with his telephone number or address; (*c*) the skip is removed as soon as practicable after it has been filled; (*d*) each of the conditions of the permission is complied with. Section 139 provides penalties for breach of the control.

5 Waste land

Builders may have a land bank and leave such land undeveloped and in an untidy condition. The same problem can arise when a building estate is developed in phases, and only some of the houses have been constructed. Such waste land if not kept tidy can become very unsightly, particularly to adjoining residents. A remedy is made available under s 65(1) of the Town and Country Planning Act 1971 (as amended by para 16 of Sched 15 to the Local Government, Planning and Land Act 1980) which provides that if it appears to a local planning authority that the amenity of any part of their area, or of any adjoining area, is seriously injured by the condition of any garden, vacant site or other open land in their area, then, subject to any directions given by the Secretary of State, the authority may serve on the owner and occupier of the land a notice requiring such steps for abating the injury as may be specified in the notice to be taken within such period as may be so specified (ie not less than twenty-eight days: s 65(2)). There appears to be no reason why the expression 'vacant site or other open land' should not apply to undeveloped building land. The penalty for non-compliance with a notice is a fine not exceeding £200 (s 104(2) as amended by para 13 of the Schedule to the Local Government and Planning (Amendment) Act 1981). By s 107(1) the local planning authority may if the notice is ignored enter the land and take any steps required by the notice and may recover from the person who is then the owner of the land any expenses reasonably incurred by them in doing so. Any expenses incurred by the owner or occupier and any sums paid by the owner of any land in respect of expenses incurred by the local planning authority in taking the steps required shall be deemed to be incurred or paid for the use and at the request of the person who caused or permitted the land to come to be in the condition in which it was when the notice was served (s 107(2)).

By s 105(1) there is a right of appeal against a notice at any time within the period specified in the notice as the period at the end of which it is to take effect. The grounds for appeal are:

(*a*) that the condition of the land does not seriously injure the amenity of any part of the area of the local planning authority who served the notice, or of any adjoining area;

(*b*) that the condition of the land is attributable to, and as such results in the ordinary course of events from, the carrying on of operations or a use of land which is not in contravention of planning control;

(*c*) that the land does not constitute a garden, vacant site or other open land;

(*d*) that the requirements of the notice exceed what is necessary for preventing the condition of the land from seriously injuring the amenity of any part of the area of the local planning authority who served the notice, or of any adjoining area;

(*e*) that the period specified in the notice as the period within which any steps required by the notice are to be taken is unreasonable.

The notice is of no effect pending the final determination or withdrawal of the appeal (s 105(3)). Appeal is made to the magistrates' court acting for the petty sessions area in which the land in question is situate (s 105(2)). There is a right of further appeal from the magistrates' court to the crown court by the appellant or the local planning authority (s 106).

6 Development land tax

(a) Section 18 exemption

There is an important exemption to development land tax which is designed to protect builders from an unexpected rise in the value of land held by them. Section 18(1) of the Development Land Tax Act 1976 provides that on the *deemed* disposal of a relevant interest in land (ie the commencement of a project of material development as defined by s 2) development land tax shall not be chargeable on any realised development value accruing to the person who is the owner of the relevant interest at the time of the disposal if the Board are satisfied that the following two conditions set out in s 18(2) are fulfilled:

(*a*) that the owner acquired the relevant interest within the period of three years ending on the date of the deemed disposal (disregarding for this purpose any acquisition on the occasion of an earlier deemed disposal and re-acquisition); and

(*b*) that if the project, the beginning of which is the occasion of the deemed disposal, had been begun immediately after the relevant interest was so acquired, no significant amount of realised development value would have accrued to the owner on the deemed disposal occurring immediately before the project began. However for disposals occurring after 9 March 1981 the condition in s 18(2)(*b*) includes the assumption that the law at the time of the acquisition of the relevant interest had been the same as it was at the date when the project began (s 131(*a*), (2) of the Finance Act 1981). For the purpose of paragraph (*b*) in any case where the owner acquired the relevant interest before the appointed day (ie 1 August 1976: s 47(1)), it shall be assumed that the appointed day fell (and the Act was in force) before the time of his acquisition.

There is a procedure laid down by s 18(3) to ascertain whether the Board (ie the Commissioners of Inland Revenue) are satisfied that the conditions have been fulfilled. If a project of material development is proposed and before that project is begun, the owner of an interest in that land makes an application to the Board and furnishes to the Board such information as they may require the Board shall notify the owner whether, if the project were to be begun forthwith, they would or would not be satisfied that the two conditions would be fulfilled with respect to that interest and that project. Any notification of clearance given by the Board pursuant to s 18(3) after 9 March 1981 will be on the assumption that there will be no change in the law between the date of the application and the commencement of the project (s 131(1)(*b*), (2) of the Finance Act 1981). Application is made on DLT form 306 to The Controller, Development Land Tax Office, Inland Revenue, Corporation House, 73/75 Albert Road, Middlesborough, Cleveland TS1 2RY. If the Board are satisfied that the conditions have been fulfilled they will notify the owner giving details of his name, the interest to which the notification relates and the date on which the person concerned acquired that interest and the project to which the notification relates (s 18(4)). Where (*a*) such a notification has been given, and (*b*) the project commences within the period of three years from the date specified in the notification of the date of acquisition, and (*c*) immediately before the beginning of that project, there is a deemed disposal of the interest to which the notice relates, development land tax shall not be chargeable (s 18(5)). For failure to furnish full information to the Board see s 18(6). It will be noted that the exemption applies even though no notification has been applied for; clearly, however, it is advisable to obtain such notification, in practice.

(b) Residential development of land held as stock in trade

To encourage builders to start residential development the base C value of 115 per cent referred to in s 5(1)(*c*) of the Development Land Tax Act 1976 has been amended. Section 129(2), (3) of the Finance Act 1981 introduces a new base value and provides that where on or after 10 March 1981 there is a *deemed* disposal of an interest in land held by the chargeable person as stock in trade and the project of material development which gives rise to the deemed disposal consists wholly or mainly of the construction or adaptation of a building or buildings for use as one or more private dwellings, the base C value is to be 150 per cent of the aggregate of the cost of the chargeable person's acquisition of the interest and of any expenditure on improvements; and for the purposes of the subsection an interest in land is held by a chargeable person as stock in trade if, had he sold that interest on the date of deemed disposal, the proceeds of sale would have been taken into account in computing the profits or gains of a trade carried on by him.

7 Retentions

A purchaser may on completion seek to retain part of the purchase monies because, for example, the property is not yet fully completed or there is an outstanding liability for road charges. Indeed, the purchaser's mortgagee may insist on such retention before agreeing to release the mortgage monies. Clearly a builder will wish to avoid such retention since a considerable amount of capital can be tied up in this manner. Furthermore, such retentions are notoriously difficult to collect even though the reason for their imposition has long since been satisfied. A compromise will therefore have to be effected between the two parties. A possible solution is for the retention monies to be deposited in a building society or bank in the joint names of the vendor and purchaser with the vendor receiving the interest from such deposit: neither party can then obtain payment of the monies without the consent of the other. If such method is adopted the reasons for retention and deposit must be clearly established in correspondence between the respective solicitors.

8 Ministry circulars

A number of circulars have been issued relating to building land over the years by both the Ministry of Housing and Local Government and the Department of the Environment, and set out below are some which may prove of assistance to the practitioner.

(a) Ministry of Housing and Local Government

44/61 Surface development in coal mining areas; 5/68 The use of conditions in planning permissions; 94/69 Surface water run off from development.

(b) Department of the Environment

132/72 Planning applications for residential development affecting the proposed line of a trunk road; 24/75 Housing—Needs and action; 44/78 Private sector land—Requirements and supply; 4/79 Memorandum on structure and local plans; 9/80 Land for private house-building; 22/80 Development control—Policy and practice and in particular Annex A — Planning permission for private sector house-building.

Appendix

Precedents

1 Option to purchase freehold land with variation to provide for conduct of a planning appeal

AN AGREEMENT made this   day of   19   BETWEEN
            (hereinafter called 'the Grantor') of the one part
and   (hereinafter called 'the Grantee') of the other part

WHEREAS the property described in the Schedule hereto is vested in the Grantor and the Grantor has agreed to grant the Grantee an option to purchase the said property for an estate in unencumbered fee simple in possession for the consideration and upon the terms hereinafter set out

NOW THEREFORE IT IS AGREED AND DECLARED as follows:

1 IN consideration of the sum of £   now paid by the Grantee to the Grantor (the receipt whereof the Grantor hereby acknowledges) and of the undertakings on the part of the Grantee hereinafter contained the Grantor hereby grants the Grantee the option of purchasing the said property described in the Schedule hereto for an estate in unencumbered fee simple in possession at the price of £

2 THE said option shall be exercisable by notice in writing to the Grantor at any time within   from the date hereof (hereinafter called 'the option period') or any extension thereof under clause 11 hereof

3 IF the said option shall be exercised by the Grantee in the manner aforesaid the Grantor shall sell the said property to the Grantee for the said estate and free from all restrictions (other than restrictions necessarily imposed in order to comply with conditions acceptable to the Grantee attached to any planning permission already obtained at the date hereof or hereafter to be obtained in connection with the said property) at the said price of £   upon the terms hereinafter mentioned

4 UPON the exercise of the said option the Grantee shall pay to the Grantor's solicitors   as stakeholders the sum of £
by way of deposit on the said sale

5 THE date for completion shall unless otherwise agreed in writing be the first working day after the expiration of   from the date of the exercise of the said option

6 THE Grantor shall convey as beneficial owner and supply to the Grantee a good and marketable title of not less than fifteen years [*amend as appropriate for registered land*]

7 THE contract for sale shall incorporate [*insert appropriate Conditions of Sale*] so far as the same are not varied by or inconsistent with the terms of this Agreement

8 VACANT possession will be given on completion

9 THE Grantee undertakes that he will within   from the date hereof at his own cost and expense prepare and lodge with the relevant planning authority an application or applications for outline planning permission to develop the said property for the purposes of   and will pursue every such application with all reasonable speed and diligence

10 THE Grantor undertakes that he will at the request and cost of the Grantee forthwith and from time to time execute and do all necessary consents acts and things to facilitate the making and granting of such outline planning permission and will at all times at the request and cost of the Grantee support the Grantee in making and pursuing every such application in all its stages including any appeal against refusal of or conditions attached to any planning permissions.

11 IF an appeal against the refusal of the Grantee's application for outline planning permission or conditional grant of outline planning permission has been lodged with the appropriate minister before the expiration of the option period and no decision on such appeal has been made by the appropriate minister before the expiration of the option period then the period during which the said option may be exercised by the Grantee in manner aforesaid shall be extended to the   day after the date of the decision letter of the appropriate minister in respect of such appeal

12 FOR the purposes of the Perpetuities and Accumulations Act 1964 the perpetuity period applicable to this Agreement shall be a period of twenty one years from the date of this Agreement.

13 THE provisions of section 196 of the Law of Property Act 1925 as amended by the Recorded Delivery Service Act 1962 shall apply to any notice served under this Agreement

14 IF notice to exercise the option shall not be given within the option period (or extended period thereof) then the Grantee shall remove any registration entered in the HM Land Charges Registry or HM Land Registry against the Grantor within seven days of notice to do so being given by the Grantor's solicitors to the Grantee's solicitors

15 [*Certificate of value if appropriate*]

AS WITNESS the hand of the Grantor and the hand of the Grantee the day and year first before written

THE SCHEDULE above referred to
[*To be completed*]

SIGNED by the Grantor
in the presence of:

SIGNED by the Grantee
in the presence of:

*   *   *

2 Option to acquire drainage or other easement

THIS AGREEMENT is made the   day of   19
BETWEEN   (hereinafter called 'the Intending Grantor')
of the one part and   (hereinafter called 'the Intending Grantee')
of the other part

WHEREAS:
(1) The Intending Grantor is the owner in fee simple in possession and free from incumbrances of the land edged   on the plan (hereinafter called 'the plan') annexed hereto
(2) The Intending Grantee is the owner in fee simple in possession and free from incumbrances of the land edged   on the plan
(3) The Intending Grantor has agreed to grant to the Intending Grantee an option to acquire the rights as hereinafter defined to lay a sewer or drain beneath the surface of the said land edged   on the plan the course of such proposed sewer or drain being shown on the plan by a black line between the points marked   [*adapt if other type of easement required*]

NOW IT IS HEREBY AGREED AND DECLARED as follows:

1 IN consideration of the sum of £   now paid by the Intending Grantee to the Intending Grantor (the receipt whereof the Intending Grantor hereby acknowledges) the Intending Grantor hereby grants to the Intending Grantee the option of acquiring the rights as hereinafter defined and upon the terms hereinafter set out
2 THE option shall be exercisable by notice in writing to the Intending Grantor at any time within   from the date hereof which shall be the option period applicable to this Agreement for the purposes of the Perpetuities and Accumulations Act 1964
3 IF the said option shall be exercised by the Intending Grantee in manner aforesaid the Intending Grantor shall in consideration of the sum

of £   paid to him grant unto the Intending Grantee and his successors in title the owners and occupiers of the property shown on the said plan and thereon edged   and his and their respective servants and licensees the rights set out in the form of Deed contained in the Schedule hereto

4 THE date for completion of the grant of the said rights shall unless otherwise agreed in writing be the first working day after the expiration of   from the date of the exercise of the said option

5 THE Intending Grantor shall supply to the Intending Grantee a good and marketable title of not less than fifteen years in relation to the rights granted by the said Deed [*amend as appropriate in the case of registered land*]

6 THE contract shall incorporate [*insert appropriate Conditions of Sale*] so far as the same are not varied by or inconsistent with the terms of this Agreement

7 THE provisions of section 196 of the Law of Property Act 1925 as amended by the Recorded Delivery Service Act 1962 shall apply to any notice served under this Agreement

8 [*Certificate of value if appropriate*]

AS WITNESS the hand of the Intending Grantor and the hand of the Intending Grantee the day and year first before written

THE SCHEDULE hereinbefore referred to
[*Incorporate Deed of Grant of Easement*]

*   *   *

3 Clause in contract for condition precedent upon outline planning consent being obtained with variations to allow for conduct of a planning appeal within a limited period

(*a*) This Agreement is conditional upon the Purchaser obtaining outline planning permission (hereinafter called 'planning permission') to develop the property hereby contracted to be sold as   within a period of   from the date hereof either free of conditions or subject to such conditions as in his absolute discretion are acceptable to the Purchaser PROVIDED ALWAYS that in the event of the initial application for planning permission being refused by the appropriate local planning authority and appeal against refusal of the Purchaser's application for planning permission being lodged with the appropriate minister in accordance with the terms of this Agreement the said period of   shall be extended to the   day after the date of the decision letter of the appropriate minister in respect of such appeal.

(*b*) The Purchaser shall within   from the date hereof apply to the appropriate planning authority for planning permission to develop the land hereby contracted to be sold for the purposes of developing the same as

(*c*) The Purchaser agrees that within   days of such application he will notify the Vendor's solicitors of the submission of the planning application (*d*) If on the initial application to the local or other appropriate planning authority the application for planning permission is refused (whether expressly in writing or by default of planning decision by the local planning authority pursuant to section 37 of the Town and Country Planning Act 1971 or any subsequent re-enactment or modification thereof) or granted subject to conditions which are unacceptable to the Purchaser he may at his absolute discretion appeal to the appropriate minister against such refusal of planning permission or unacceptable conditions within a period of   from the date of this Agreement provided always that in the event of the Purchaser failing to appeal within the said period of   this Agreement shall at the expiration of that period be null and void save that the Vendor's solicitors shall forthwith on the failure of the Purchaser to give notice of appeal within the said period refund to the Purchaser on the expiration of the said period the said deposit of £   without interest

(*e*) In the event of planning permission as aforesaid being granted free of conditions or granted subject to conditions which are acceptable to the Purchaser either on the initial application for planning permission or on appeal to the appropriate minister completion of this Agreement shall take place within a period of   of the receipt in writing by the purchaser of the planning permission as aforesaid being granted by the local planning authority on the initial application or in the case of such planning permission being granted by the appropriate minister on appeal within a period of   from the date of the decision letter of the appropriate minister in respect of such appeal

(*f*) In the event of planning permission being granted on appeal subject to conditions which are unacceptable to the Purchaser the Purchaser shall within a period of   from the date of the decision letter of the appropriate minister serve notice in writing to the effect that the conditions are unacceptable whereupon this Agreement shall be null and void and upon service of such notice the Vendor's solicitors shall forthwith refund to the Purchaser the said deposit of £   without interest

(*g*) In the event of planning permission being refused on appeal this Agreement shall from the date of the decision letter of the appropriate minister be null and void whereupon the Vendor's solicitors shall forthwith refund to the Purchaser the said deposit of £   without interest

(*h*) On the refusal or granting of planning permission the Purchaser hereby agrees to provide the Vendor with a copy of such planning permission or refusal within   of the receipt in writing by the Purchaser of such planning permission or refusal

(*i*) The provisions of section 196 of the Law of Property Act 1925 as amended by the Recorded Delivery Service Act 1962 shall apply to any notice served under this Agreement.

*   *   *

4 Clause in contract for condition subsequent upon outline planning consent being obtained with variation to allow for conduct of a planning appeal within a limited period

(*a*) The date for the completion of the purchase shall be whichever is the earlier of either the   day of   19   or (i) in the case of outline planning permission (the planning permission) being granted on the initial application to the local planning authority   days after the receipt in writing by the Purchaser of the planning permission or (ii) in the case of the planning permission being granted on appeal   days from the date of the decision letter of the appropriate minister granting the planning permission in either case for the development of the land hereby contracted to be sold as [*insert details of proposed development*]

(*b*) The Purchaser shall within   from the date hereof submit to the local planning authority an application for planning permission

(*c*) If the application for planning permission is refused (whether expressly in writing or by default of planning decision by the local planning authority pursuant to section 37 of the Town and Country Planning Act 1971 or any subsequent re-enactment or modification thereof) on the initial application for planning permission to the appropriate local planning authority the Purchaser shall forthwith lodge an appeal against refusal of planning permission and shall bear the expense of such appeal and prosecute such appeal with all due speed and diligence

(*d*) If planning permission has been refused on appeal prior to the said   day of   19   or if completion has not taken place by the said   day of   19   either party may by notice in writing rescind this contract whereupon the contract will cease to have effect save that the Vendor shall forthwith repay to the Purchaser the deposit paid pursuant to the terms of this Agremeent without interest

(*e*) The provisions of section 196 of the Law of Property Act 1925 as amended by the Recorded Delivery Service Act 1962 shall apply to any notice served under this Agreement.

*   *   *

Index